DIGGING for MOTHER'S BONES

A GUIDE TO UNEARTHING TRUE FEMININE NATURE

Coco Oya Cienna-Rey

WOMANCRAFT PUBLISHING

Copyright © 2024 Coco Oya Cienna-Rey.

All rights reserved. No part of this publication may be reproduced, distributed, or transmitted in any form or by any means, including photocopying, recording, or other electronic or mechanical methods, without the prior written permission of the publisher, except in the case of brief quotations embodied in critical reviews and certain other non-commercial uses permitted by copyright law.

Published by Womancraft Publishing, 2024
womancraftpublishing.com

ISBN 978-1-910559-97-0

Digging for Mother's Bones is also available in ebook format: ISBN 978-1-910559-99-4

Cover image © Dorrie Joy

Permission to reproduce Extract from "Message from Brigid", Siobhán Mac Mahon (2020) @siobhanmacmahonpoet

Womancraft Publishing is committed to sharing powerful new women's voices, through a collaborative publishing process. We are proud to midwife this work, however the story, the experiences and the words are the authors' alone. A percentage of Womancraft Publishing profits are invested back into the environment reforesting the tropics (via TreeSisters) and forward into the community.

The information provided is intended to complement, not replace, the advice of your own doctor or other health care professional, whom you should always consult about your individual needs and any symptoms that may require diagnosis or medical attention and before starting or stopping any medication or starting any new course of treatment, exercise regime or diet.

Printed in Ireland by Carraig Print Litho Press, Cork.

PRAISE

Digging for Mother's Bones is a profound exploration of the feminine essence and its deeply rooted connections within our lives. It's a healing balm for the collective feminine psyche, eloquently navigating the terrain of motherhood, womanhood and the sacredness of life.

The book is an essential read for those yearning to reconnect with their inner wisdom and to honor the interconnectivity of life as seen through the lens of the Divine Feminine. It is a manifesto for transformation and an invitation to a deeper communion with our true nature. The journey Coco lays out is one of profound awakening and healing, necessary for anyone looking to mend the fractures of a disconnected world and find solace in the arms of the Great Mother.

Astara Jane Ashley, MA, CEO and publisher of Flower of Life Press, book midwife and ordained priestess

Coco Oya Cienna-Rey is a true oracular voice for The Great Mother, anchoring the reclamation of the wild, sensual, embodied and future ancient feminine.

Digging for Mother's Bones is a manifesto to counter the hijack and censorship of womb, body, heart through the revelatory pathways of raw sensuality, mysticism, and rebellion.

Reading Coco Oya Cienna-Rey's work is a refuge for those who have heard the clarion call to return to the initiations of dark fertile wisdom of the feminine. We are blessed to have Cienna-Rey's prophetic and lyrical voice alive amongst us.

Caroline Seckinger of Her Eternal Ceremonial Knives, artist, author and ceremonial guide

A powerful, unapologetic call to remember the true essence and potency of the Mother. In a world that seems increasingly determined to abuse, obfuscate, deny and distort Woman's inherent embodied intelligence, Coco Oya Cienna-Rey's voice is clear and welcome balm.

Her writing asks us to enter a process of descent through the real, raw, radiant body of ourselves that delivers us home to our Mother wisdom. Can we process our trauma and move through our pain, vulnerability and personal stories, to uncover the original seeds of knowing buried deep in the marrow of ourselves? Digging for Mother's Bones offers a compelling mixture of personal story woven with teachings, insights and embodied exercises to help you do just that.

Carly Mountain, author of *Descent & Rising: Women's Stories & the Embodiment of the Inanna Myth*

Coco Oya shares her journey from a place of unexamined intergenerational trauma to a life of full and courageous exploration of shadow and pain. She takes us along in the discovery of how the Divine Feminine has been diminished and demonized, and how the fears for survival have forced women to deny their true power. She bravely leads us into a mapping of the shadow places with helpful exercises and a desire for full embodiment. I had a lightbulb moment in understanding that seeking higher realms of consciousness does not require escaping the body but rather, requires that we deepen our physical attentiveness and become more embodied. Her life, her journey, and this book are an inspiration for us all.

**Gina Martin, author of the *When She Wakes* series
(Sisters of the Solstice Moon, Walking the Threads of Time, She Is Here)**

Coco's raw honesty in sharing her story is deeply touching, and allows one to grieve, rage, laugh and celebrate with her. It also creates a space within which we can all step into a profound honouring of ourselves, our mothers, our mother lines and of Her, the Great Mother.

Coco is truly a siren for the Mother and Digging for Mother's Bones is the kind of medicine that our world so desperately needs right now.

Emmi Mutale, womb healer, author, founder of Feminine Revered, host of the 'Sacred Feminine Power' podcast and the Return to the Mother World speaker series

Coco Oya Cienna-Rey speaks of the Mother, the Goddess, in a way that only a true initiate of the sacred feminine can. She presents an invitation to do the work, to do the reflecting, as the key to return home to the masculine and feminine within us all.

She weaves the story of her own sacred journey as a woman, mother, and healer, granting us intimate insight into what it looks like to surrender to the call of the Goddess and to become an Oracle of the Divine Mother. Following along as she outlines transformational spiritual practices to tap into the wisdom of the Goddess served to anchor me more deeply into my womb and into my own calling.

This has very quickly become one of my favorite books about the feminine, the Goddess, and the Mother.

Tiara Shardé, oracle, founder of The Pussy Portal and Embodying the Goddess Temple & Mystery School

A heartfelt, authentic and powerful guide to unearthing true feminine nature, Coco's book is inspiring and timely. Rooted in her lived-experience, every word she writes is a resonant call from the deep feminine to awaken the embodied wisdom within every one of us. Essential reading for anyone who wishes to honour life, earth and The Great Mother whose time is now.

Umā Dinsmore-Tuli PhD, author of *Yoni Shakti, A Woman's Guide to Power, Freedom through Yoga and Tantra* and *Nidrā Shakti: an Illustrated Encyclopaedia of Yoga Nidrā*

This work is a timely, precious and necessary attunement to the archetype of Mother, who was suppressed by patriarchy, religious dogma and pathology. Coco's voice beckons the reader deeper into the feminine intelligences of emotion and intuition. Supporting them gracefully with practices to reclaim and balance the fullness of their humanity.

This is not just a book, it's a sacred journey of reclamation.

Blessed be.

Rainbow Goddess, matricentric feminist researcher, mushroom shamaness and creator of the podcast, 'Motherhood: Rawful But True'

This book is dedicated to my daughters, my granddaughter and the memory of my mother.

This is for you who hear the call of the Mother as she guides us home.

Together we are resurrecting Her bones.

CONTENTS

Opening	1
Part One: REAL	11
My Mother	12
The Mother	28
The Mother Codes	31
The Mother Wound	35
Welcoming Back the Mother	43
Part Two: RAW	47
Surrender	49
The Descent	52
Navigating the Shadow	55
The Dark Night of the Soul	57
Death	63
Part Three: RADIANT	71
The Potency of Woman	73
Boundaries	77
Claiming Our Power	80
Intuition	85
Initiation	90
Sexual Energy	95

Tantra	102
Intimate Connection	108
Womb	116
Birth	122
Mothering	124
Learning to Manage Our Energy	129
Feminine Flow	131
An End to Struggle	135
Embodying Her	137
Closing: EVOLUTION	**145**
Reclaiming the Fierce Feminine	146
Remembering	150
Mother World	152
Being a Force of Nature	152
Raising Her Temples	154
Metamorphosis	157
Our Ancient Future	158
Acknowledgements	161
Author's Note	163
About the Author	167
About the Artist	168

Fragment

One day a voice spoke to me
in the language of silence;
my body answered
and I was undone.
Return to the land
of your belonging, She said
dig up the bones
of the forgotten,
follow the old dreaming paths,
the truth has been trapped
in a sarcophagus of soil and silence,
but there is a new story
more beautiful than anything
you could possibly imagine
and the time has come
for it to be heard.

From "Message from Brigid", Siobhán Mac Mahon (2020)

OPENING

Opening

There is a deep wellspring in life. And that wellspring is the Mother. We, as a collective, have become separated from Her true essence. She has been relegated into the background of society; Her potency watered down. We have become depleted of Her nutrients and as a result the world is in severe imbalance. This book is a guide to evoke the remembrance and embrace of Her essence. A remembrance of a time when we naturally received from life and life was seen as sacred.

This book shares a forgotten language of the feminine that was forced underground and now is rising beneath our feet, seeping into our flesh and bones. It is the wisdom I wish I had received as I grew into a young woman and contemplated becoming a mother.

The hidden language of the Mother anchors us back into an ancient lineage. A deep knowing that we are and always will be an aspect of Her. So much of what it means to fully embrace the full frequency of womanhood and motherhood has been erased or distorted in our collective psyche. It has distracted us from being our true selves and led us down many blind alleyways in search of deeper meaning. The words within this book are designed to bring you back to a sense of alignment with the feminine and strip back the layers that have held you in a detached state from your innate knowing of Her. This book is dedicated to the Mother in all of us.

*

Within these pages is an exploration of our maternal lineage, our bodies and how the essence of the Mother weaves into both. On a personal level there were many times when my journey as a mother were shady and shoddy. I played the sacrificial martyred mother so well. I blamed my life for my lack of freedom. I thought I had been hard-done-by and somehow swindled. I share some of my story with you in these pages by way of example, and with the intention of showing how things can transform when we decide to let Her in. So much of my story isn't easy to share, but it is necessary. The crisis points we are at today in the world are a macro reflection of the micro journey I took to become a carrier of the Mother's essence as medicine. She will always bring us back, even if that means we are taken into the dark belly of the underworld to know that new life can only come from being held and resurrected in the dark.

I write for those who have felt like seekers all their lives, looking for that magical pill to take the pain away. For those who have been left wanting, longing, yearning for something far deeper than they have been told is possible. I am here for those who have known all along that there is something more to life than what we see with the naked eye, yet have been unable to touch it. This book is for the truth seekers, the inquisitive questioners who have been searching for a place to call home.

*

This book is not for the mind. It is for the realm of feeling: to sense into the depths of magic that lie within. It is for the feminine soul. It is a celebration of the female body. It isn't about me infusing you with my knowing, it is about you opening up to your unique relationship with Her. Let my story, my experience be an activation of your own truth. Some of what I have written here may not make sense to you on a mental level, yet it will make sense to your heart and body. Take note of any sensations you feel. Write down your responses. Chart what arises as you go.

We hold in the depths of our being the feminine quality of longing, a depth of relating from deep within our womb and heart, a longing to merge. A soul calling that breaks the heart open into rapturous song: the path of the mystic. But most of us have been taught to live cut off from the neck down, tethered to logic and separated from our innate feminine gifts. Within these pages I weave reasons as to why we become separated from or abandon our magic in order to feel like we belong, yet in doing so we disconnect from the mysteries of life. The unseen world has been demonised, and those that feel it and know it to be more real than what we tangibly can see have been judged harshly for standing in that knowing. This book is a testimony to the power of the feminine that comes to your aid when you call. Or when She calls you: The Mother of all Life.

This book is a manifesto that lets you know that your time has come. The reclamation of your magic is so needed. It is time to stand up and bring all that you know out of the closet. The Mother is here to support your awakening. We are being called by Her. It is time to let the sap of Her rise up like liquid gold, up through your feet, as an activation, so that you can take your wisdom out into the streets. Let Her rising sap be the elixir, the healing balm that helps you remove your limiting beliefs and gives you the courage to practice your gifts and magic openly and show the world that you are a woman who is here to seed a new world. It is time to use all that has been turned against us and alchemise it into endless fuel for our own growth.

This book is a remembering from whence we came. A reminder, if you need it, that we are each a drop in the ocean, each a tiny part of the vastness of Her, and therefore, we each carry a concentrated fragment of Her in our bodies. Our womb is a microcosm of the Cosmic Womb. Our body, a reflection of the body of the Earth. Our blood the same as the rivers. Our knowing the same as her gnosis. When we lean into Her, into the field of Her existence, we can reconnect to the ancient codes of the feminine. In doing so we connect to our lineage of the ancient ones and to that of our ancestors: they have knowledge and wisdom for us to aid us through these times.

This book is for every woman who has felt a sense of waiting and feels the ripples of new life coming in, so that you know that your very existence has been about birthing a deeper knowing to assist in these times. It is for the hidden mystic locked away inside of you, the places where you have overridden and ignored your intuition. It is for all those who have had their soul fragmented by trauma or abuse and find themselves in the depths of their shadowy darkness, wondering if there is a way out. Now is the time to rebirth your magic, because on the other side of our suppression and fear is pure joy and a feeling of wholeness. Now is the time for your evolutionary remembrance, for you to move beyond the life you have been living. Let the priestess, warrior, shaman, witch, mother, lover, oracle, seer, creator inside of you come to the forefront so that you can walk in the world as your true self and relinquish the slow death you have been living. The magic that lives inside you is waiting to be met. And your relationship with the Mother is central to your core. She pulses through you, whether you are aware or not. She is the blueprint to your soul.

The feminine creates order out of chaos. She is stirring the earth beneath our feet. Preparing us for the next steps in our evolutionary journey. She is lifting the carpet so we can see what was swept under there and shaking loose our collusion with silence. Some may find Her ways healing; others will feel provoked. Yet all will be forever changed from Her rising. For She is a mirror for the world. She cannot be measured or controlled. She travels far beyond the realms of the thinking mind. Her inner sight defies logic. She is a landline to the great void, a conduit for deep truths. She is service to all life. Her ability to see behind what is being presented brings cosmic order in sight. May your eyes and mind be opened through Her wild sensual nature.

Language

Although this book is unapologetically written with a female-centric viewpoint, I wholeheartedly welcome anyone who wishes to tap into the depth of the feminine within them. We are at a time in our evolution where the feminine rising needs all of Her devotees in attendance. We are removing the distance and separation between the sexes. We are all birthed from the womb of woman and originate from the same cluster of cells. Whomever She calls to this path, you will know, you will feel the pull to build a new world that has the feminine infused within it. You know you are here to be a vessel of service to Her. Find within these pages transmissions to bring you back to a cellular remembrance of why you came to this earthly plane at this time.

I speak from the perspective of heterosexual relationships because it is how I have lived most of my life. Yet, the dynamics of our inner masculine and feminine run throughout all couples regardless of their sexual orientation: it is about the flow of energetics between the two rather than the physical pairing. I have been in a same-sex relationship and we still had the same forces at work within that pairing. One erring more towards the masculine dynamic and the other taking more of the feminine aspects, until we learnt to bring the balance between the two within ourselves. Throughout the book please keep this in mind when reading about the masculine and feminine undercurrents at play within our relating and the wider field of our individual, social and cultural lived experience. We all carry the seed of divinity which is the masculine and feminine essence united.

When I speak of 'woman' in an exalted way through these pages, know that it is not to place one sex over another or to have an air of superiority either. It is simply that at this evolutionary time, the body of woman has a specific role to play which involves the unique living technology of her womanly vessel. What I mean when I use the term 'woman' is a biological female that has (or has had) a womb and pussy. So much of the power of women comes from these two power points when connected to the heart. I believe it is one of the main reasons we have been conditioned to have little or no real relationship with these body parts and why they have been so vilified throughout our distorted patriarchal history.

Women have an innate ability to connect to otherworldly realms by the nature of the design of their bodies and their ability to bring in and birth souls. The energetics of this differ in the male body, although I do believe they can have a similar energetic imprint in the lower abdomen – the seat of where our power resides – in Traditional Chinese Medicine and martial arts it is called the *dantian*.

What I define as a woman is not up for debate. I am here to honour, speak to and ignite the remembrance of her sacred nature.

You may also be asking why I use the term 'pussy' above all else when referring to the sacred portal that lies between our thighs. Especially when it is so often felt as such an activating word. I use it primarily for that very reason, as an activation and remembrance of the connection to the root of the body. To awaken your inner enquiry as to why there is so much controversy around female genitalia: the very place where we as women birth our species into the world. Why would that be? That very question sums up why I use it and just how disconnected we have become from the Mother.

Many I know in the New Age world use the word *yoni* (a Sanskrit word for female genitalia that translates as origin, source, or spring – and includes the vulva and vagina). For me, pussy is separate from womb. It has a whole energetic blueprint and purpose unto itself. Pussy is the portal, the gateway into our inner sanctum and is a reminder that it holds unfathomable power and has a completely different energetic imprint than using the word yoni. During your reading of the book use whatever term makes you feel comfortable.

Whatever word you use, please note that on a physical level they both lead to the deeper inner chambers: the cervix and uterus that are the energetic doorways to connecting to the inner depths of your being and to the cosmos. As we move through the book, see if you can let the potency of this knowing be a constant reminder that you are giving your precious body parts a voice and that this root is the home that connects us to the Mother. We root into her from this space. It is the portal through which life is birthed as well as birthing our creations out into the world.

Trauma

Please note that I refer to my own childhood and sexual trauma throughout the pages in this book. Our world is one defined by trauma. Individual and collective. We have created a culture that has trauma embedded within its very fabric. Trauma happens when we are taught to avoid, ignore or escape our pain. When we learn to stop feeling.

When you are raised in trauma, life becomes a series of devastating events. You get used to being taken advantage of. You get used to life being hard. You get used to having to struggle for real connection. You push life away. Life becomes a constant threat and you will challenge it at every turn or run and hide from it. Abuse messes with your sense of self on all levels. You lose the ability to trust yourself and make good judgements. It takes a lot of self-growth to begin to trust your gut once more. Because when you are taught to override your deepest knowing, to close your eyes to what has happened to you, you learn to stop believing in yourself. We are conditioned from a young age not to be centred in our own knowing; we get taught to follow the rules of those around us. And in doing so we slowly lose our ability to steer our lives from the inside. We end up building walls around us, unable to claim our true needs because for the majority of our lives we are given what we don't want.

Trauma always seeks resolution and gets louder until we choose to acknowledge it and give it the love that it seeks. I ignored my own trauma for many years, I did not heed the warning that unresolved trauma causes chaos and causes you to inflict pain on others.

It is my intention in this book when I talk about trauma to ignite an activation of truth in you to awaken your light. But by its very nature when we shine light, we naturally illuminate our dark spots too. Be sure to read with care, and seek help and assistance if needed whether through a therapist or a trusted friend. Take care of yourself and hold yourself with the tender love of the Mother as you allow the gentle touch of awareness to begin to soften the places you may have hardened in yourself.

Structure of the Book

This book provides a detailed understanding of reclaiming our relationship with the Mother on a global, individual and energetic level. It weaves my own personal story of coming into full relationship with the Mother, my own story of healing – as mother and daughter – with exercises to help you embody and practice what you learn in the book and transmissions from the Mother.

Within the first section of the book, we explore our stories of who we are as mothers and daughters, how we have experienced these relationships in our own lives. We learn about the mother wound and meet the Mother.

In the second part, we dive into the unravelling of self, the process of coming undone. In this time of grand unravelling, every ideology of separation and segregation is intensifying. It can feel scary and disorientating. But what if you knew that this is necessary, and that in the midst of the chaos and destruction, new life is birthing?

In the third part, we look at the energy of the feminine as it is expressed in our bodies, as it is expressed in birth, sex, mothering, intuition and devotion. We move beyond the small fear-based stories of our culture, and explore how we can embrace and embody the true feminine in our lives. We look at ways to bring Her out into the world through our bodies and actions.

We finish by reflecting on the bigger picture: the next evolutionary phase of humanity beyond man-made directives and laws. This is the time of Her revival: how can we best serve it?

This book is an outpouring of love from the Mother to you. I suggest you read it as a living breathing text. Much of the book is a transmission from Her. Let what wants to move through you do so, as you feel the truth penetrate you through the pages of this book. Allow the sensations of the body be felt, and know that they won't always make sense to the mind. Engage your imagination, it is an ally that is so often given a bad rap. Your sensitivity plays a significant role in reigniting your erotic and sensual nature, both are key facets that awaken our connection back to the Mother. Your imagination takes you beyond the physical and elevates your ability to tune into the more subtle realms of life. Be gentle with yourself as your awareness grows. You are growing a new muscle of expanded awareness. Ultimately, with the aid of this book, you are entering into a remembrance of the true essence of Mother beyond the myth of Her. She is longing for you.

You are no longer alone.

A little on Activations and Transmissions before we begin

My role in this life is to be a transmission for Her, to reclaim myself as 'a siren of the Mother', to raise awareness around the love She wishes to impart to us and share how that can help restore balance between the masculine and feminine elements of life that have been drastically out of balance. I have connected to the depths of the Mother and know that Her love is unbounded. I am here to share that with you. Through these pages you will be guided to Her. She will show you the way to your own heart.

Like mycelium we are all energetically connected to the umbilical cord of the Mother. Our connection to Her is symbiotic: a mutual exchange. It is a relationship that will set you free from the bindings of outdated beliefs and into the limitless nature of life. However, be warned: this is never an easy journey. All that no longer serves is stripped away. We become undone and we learn to die well. And thus, we are rebirthed through Her. So come to this book with your perfectly imperfect self as we release the old paradigm that says we are never whole. And in doing so we honour our inner children, and learn to mother ourselves and each other.

Throughout this book you will find seeds planted for your activation in the form of exercises. Know that these are keys or codes laid out as an invitation for your further exploration. At the time of writing this book I was guided to shift the way I teach and give information, thus, these exercises are an invitation to ignite a deeper knowing and a way back to following your own internal guidance.

Most of what I write here will be like a remembering to many and a recognition of some of what you have been experiencing in your own life. A confirmation that you too are being called into a deeper way of being. To understand the fleeting moments of intuition you may already have had and reassurance that the breadcrumbs left along your path have true meaning: you are being called home by Her.

I recommend keeping a journal of some kind with you as you journey with this book – glean the insights that may come, record your dreams, recognise and acknowledge any memories or communications with the ancestors that require your witness. Plus, it would be good to record any encounters you have with the essence I call the Mother. When Her energy descended on me, it was so familiar. I recognised that throughout my life the times She had already visited were precursors to Her full-blown arrival that I describe in this book. You may have remembrances as you read this book that She too has been with you for longer than you realise.

Dear Woman,

For millennia your story has been mistold.

Your multidimensionality hidden under falsehoods.

They would have you believe that you have no real value

That your position is to be submissive. To take up less room.

You have learned to contort yourself into a version of smallness

And believed that to gain any real knowing you have to fight to be seen.

When in reality you are a bridge between worlds.

The true frequency of Woman has a tone so crystal clear

That when you allow yourself to sit in its resonance

It brings you back home to the magnificence of your being.

Can you allow yourself to fully feel that in your body and bones?

Can you allow yourself to remember Her?

She is your Mother… in you, as you are in Her…

Come, remember…

PART ONE

REAL

My Mother

I cannot tell the story of Her, without telling my own story. I cannot tell my own story without telling something of my mother's story…and my daughters' stories. This is how it is. Mothers and daughters, interwoven down the motherline. All the way back to Her. My story is a version of our story.

The Great Mother has been knocking at my door for many years, but it took a near death experience for me to finally heed the call to voice what is coming through me. This is an attempt to piece together the threads that made a woman like me want to die at the age of forty-nine. And how meeting Her brought me back to life.

*

I do not know much about where I came from, the history of my ancestral lineage, the origins of my being… My story is one of lost identities and the heritage of trauma, of heartache and pain. A tale which, although unique to me, seems commonplace for so many others as well. I fought all the way through. I saw every single one of my experiences as painful and evidence of life being out to get me. I could not see the weaving of my soul's story from this time round, from my past life experiences and for the ones I was lining up to receive, or that they all held a thread for me to create my life.

It's time to strip the story back, go down into its marrow.

*

I have no idea what my mother came to learn as a sovereign soul. Having seen so many of the patterns play out in my own life, I think that her relationship with my father may have been the very thing she came to experience to evolve her soul. Even if that isn't the case and it was all just a tragedy, I know that being witness to it all helped me eventually grow. My sheer determination not to be like her, to unwind and undo the toxicity has changed my ancestral lineage for good. Seeing my mother for the woman she was, rather than who I needed her to be, enabled me to accept her path as one of pain. Forgiveness enabled me to see the bigger picture. It was more for me than it was for her. I let myself off the hook. All the energy I used to try and change her would never have made any difference anyway. Acceptance of who she was was the only way forward. If I'd have known then how her life was going to end, would I have tried to change her mind? I will never know. What I do know is that her death sent me into a dark place. A place where the real healing could start. And in opening to the vulnerability of that I got to return to the original Mother.

In so many ways my mother was the strongest and most loving woman I knew. Yet she lived a life filled with disempowerment, violence and unlived dreams. There were times I literally hated her. I hated that she didn't care for herself, it felt as though she didn't care whether she lived or died.

I could not understand what could have made a strong woman like my mother stay with an unhinged man like my father, way past the point any other rational human being would have left. My mother put all of her energy into taking care of the men in our family and not herself. She felt purposeful when needed, she was the perpetual rescuer. She stuffed her greatness and bigness down and undervalued herself. She showed me how to sacrifice, how to dampen my life force, to be subservient. It seeped into my bones, my psyche, and became part of who I was. And so I set myself up to be undernourished and utilised in relationships. I learnt to choose men that could not match my energy, but instead loved to dominate it, a pattern I saw play out in the whole of my childhood. This was a pattern I also saw play out in the wider world. The groundwork for my life was laid long before I entered this world. Patterns of distortion passed down my maternal line and infused with the imprint of my paternal line: a dangerous infusion of chaos that rocked my world.

*

I know very little of my mother's past, and what I do know seems mournful to my mind. She never talked much about her life before she came to England from Jamaica in the early 1950s, yet I knew from the yearning in her eyes that she longed to return home. She had left four of her children there in the hopes of them coming over at some later date. That never happened. Instead, she got trapped in a relationship with my father, a man with no real concern for family matters. His womanising and alcoholic ways meant their home was never a stable base. When my mother fell pregnant with my older brother, she became even more trapped in their loveless relationship and was forced to marry my father. This was something I only discovered after her death through reading a series of letters I found, which stated that her family back home in Jamaica washed their hands of her. Now stuck in the UK with a child on the way and her other children left behind, the letter said, "You made your bed, now lie in it." There are times in my life that my heart is heavy because I never got to see my mother in her full womanhood. I can only imagine how torn she felt inside. Especially when, in the early 1990s, her eldest son died unexpectedly from a brain haemorrhage. She was never the same after that. It pains me how little mothers are fully received in the world. How little support they have to be the best mother they can be.

When my mother died fifteen years ago, I felt a deep sense of abandonment and loss that I couldn't ask her vital questions about why she did the things she did or how she truly felt. I was left incomplete and had to find ways to bring some conclusion to our connection. Only now can I feel the full truth of the reasons she lived the way she did. I see her story reflected in mine as I dig into the bones of our lives here on Earth and beyond as I piece together our stories.

*

One element of my story I often hold back is the part of how my mother lost her life. It's not an easy realisation to bear witness to and it still holds many unanswered questions.

I believe my mother's life was cut short by my father. It will never be a proven fact whether he took her life – the inquest was inconclusive. Yet based on what I know, as well as what I have been told through spiritual messages from beyond the veil and my own intuitive guidance, I know her life was cut short. I also know it wasn't intentional. I am grateful to all those concerned that helped me in my search for answers – the police who investigated, as well as psychics, mediums and shamans – each of whom gave me the same answer without being prompted. The whole of that process deepened my trust and conviction in the unseen world.

I tell the story of my mother without blame and without shame. I tell it in the name of transparency. As a child so much was brushed under the carpet and it resulted in chaos and tragedy for so many in my lineage. So many, including myself, had to hide behind a façade, terrified to speak up, afraid to show the underbelly of our lives. I share not to condemn or condone my father's behaviour, but to demonstrate the harm that can be caused when our pain is not tended to…and the healing that can take place when it is.

*

It is strange what happens when you begin to allow yourself to remember. When the memories would first arise, I could feel and hear my heart pounding and blood rushing through my ears. This part of the journey was beyond challenging. The memories wouldn't always have pictures to them. So, I was often left with unexplainable sensations. I since found out that when abuse happens before our preverbal capacity, we will feel in sensations alone. Like putting together the pieces of a puzzle, I had to learn to trust my body's innate intelligence and allow it to release. They say that the memories only arise when you are ready to face them. I had to learn to gain some distance between the sensations and the visions so that I could begin to look at them with a compassionate eye.

In my case, my initial inability to have negative feelings towards my mother made me ill. It also eventually turned me into a villain. I turned against myself and dumbed myself out with alcohol, drugs and emotionally unavailable men. I squandered my energy in so many ways and hid behind anger. The me in my early twenties to mid-thirties was emotionally stunted. I never learnt emotional maturity from any of the adult relationships that were around me. In my childhood I had to grow up fast. I became Little Miss Independent. I shaped myself into the good girl, the obedient girl, who would contort herself to receive her mother's love, including sacrificing myself to abuse.

We are so conditioned in our world to believe we should only have positive feelings about our mothers. Yet we live in a world where the current paradigms set the tone for us to have a gaping hole that is filled with the mother wound. So much so that when we do have negative feelings towards our mothers it can cause great internal conflict. We turn the pain in on ourselves rather than be seen as the bad daughter. We play this game with ourselves until we get to a point where we have to start seeing that we matter. That we have a right to own our feelings.

We can't change the past, but we can mine it for gold even when the past has been horrific. Part of the process of healing the wounds of your parental relationships is that memory after memory will come flooding back. In the early stages of my healing journey, every morning I would wake up to flashbacks of the terror I faced as a child. Visions played out like movies in my mind as I began the thawing process to reinstating my feelings and sensations, as I dared to journey deeper into the hidden layers of my psyche.

I went mute for a while in my childhood: the violence I witnessed was too much for my underdeveloped mind to comprehend. I developed a belief that if I spoke up like my mother tried to, then my father would inflict the same upon me. I soon learnt that it really didn't matter whether I made a sound or not. He was an unpredictable man and anything could set him off. Yet his motto, "Children should be seen and not heard" stuck. And I learnt that sitting quietly and smiling nicely was the best strategy…for a while. Up until the time I reached puberty and I could no longer hold back the fire that was beginning to rise up from my womb when it came to injustice against our female forms.

The truth of the matter is that I never felt wanted. I was the last child birthed out of eight created by my parents' various relationships. I was a tie to my father: a tie I later found out my mother did not want. Yet, even knowing and feeling all of that, I fell into the same pattern of criticising my eldest child. It's not a pretty truth, but it was the reality at the time when, as a young new mother, I was re-traumatised into my own childhood wounding. Each milestone in my child's life triggered a remembrance of my own trauma. Yet, no one, including myself, understood what was happening to me. The language of trauma wasn't really a thing.

My relationship with my mother became a mirror to the one I had with my eldest daughter. I was both the difficult mother and the wounded daughter. I have been the person to hurt her child and I have been the hurt child. This is a difficult statement to make. It is seen as taboo to speak the truth. Yet I know it is time to break the silence and crack open the shadows around this more openly. It isn't for us to solve each other's problems, but to be a support to one another as we find our own solutions. Even when our mothers leave our lives, the wounds are still there: they live within our bones. No matter if you choose to do the work to heal or not, her legacy lives on, one way or another.

*

My connection with my mother has grown beyond the veil of death. I realise that her soul's journey is a catalyst for my own soul's awakening. In recent years I have come to unwind many things along my maternal lineage and reform them into medicine. My paternal lineage too involved a lot of inner work. It held the heaviest karmic abuse relating to power and control. My parents were the perfect toxic match for one another. So much darkness has been a heavy burden on my soul and human self. There were many times I did not know if I would make it. Yet, at each point of perceived defeat, something or someone would come into my life to remind me that life has my back.

It took until the impending threshold of my mother's death to begin to see her just as a woman who had made her choices to stay with someone who had abused her and all of her children. To have compassion and deep love for her and her path as a soul and as a woman. To recognise that she died with her longing locked in her heart.

I did not know she was going to die within a few months of that realisation. We had just come back into contact with one another after a family member saw me on the street one day and told me that my mother was not well. I had been estranged from her for about a year before that. I do not even know what changed, I just clearly remember looking at her and for a moment she wasn't my mother, she was just a woman who had had a hard life and I could give her love and hold her with compassion.

The contrast was palpable. Before that reunion, I couldn't even be in her presence without feeling hurt or getting angry. I had so much unprocessed need I couldn't feel her or myself. My inner child that longed for mother's love was ravenously hungry and running the show. That part of me saw my mother's inability to leave my father as weakness. It felt like she had abandoned all of her children. Like we had been deeply neglected rather than loved. In her way my mother did love, but it never felt enough. Underneath all my anger was grief, and until I felt that, I could never feel her full love. Underneath the anger was the fear of ending up the same as her. I almost did. And on many occasions I followed the same toxic patterns whilst all the time professing to not be like her.

My inner child often wished my mother was dead, I felt trapped and frustrated by her. But later in life it was me that I thought should die. I saw no way out from the thoughts that plagued me that I was a bad mother; and that I would never be able to take care of myself properly. As I moved into a space of reclaiming my energy, I could finally see a way to break the chain for the next generation. I no longer wanted to pass on the baton of ignoring my own needs. I knew in order to do so, the baton of being the martyr and the lack of self-care had to be put down too.

*

Our family traits can run deep. We have to be willing to look at them head-on and be in full acceptance that this too is who we are. No amount of pushing them away or trying to run from them will stop their impact in our lives. What will, is holding them with love. Admitting and feeling the full force of them within ourselves and those that we see as harming us in the past. They are part of us, whether we see that or not. What would it be like to allow yourself to feel that they are always with you? What then? How do you navigate through life when you can't run away from who you are? You realise that this is an 'and and' world and as much as you have your humanity, you also have your divinity. And you can decide which track to focus on. As souls we came to experience life in all its flavours. We cannot escape that fact. The key is to ask: What is this path and where is it leading me? What are some of these darker experiences teaching me? Who are the people that I travelled with beyond the roles they played? How can I see them through my soul's eyes?

Before I could ask myself those questions, I lived in a state of arrested development, stalled in a teenage stage for a long time, full of the psychological rejection I felt from my elders. This is a normal stage of development, but one I took to the extreme. I couldn't get out of the loop. I felt I had lost so much. The wounding of my inner child felt way too deep to let myself have any form of freedom. There were too many emotions to unravel. I had no map of how to even begin to feel freedom from my past. Yet the longing for the deeper truth underneath all that never went away.

I never learnt any form of emotional intelligence from my family. There were plenty of emotional outbursts, yet there was no real emotional expression. We threw mud at one another, we pulled each other down, all real signs that we were not truly feeling. As a child I felt so let down, but I had no understanding of the layers at play. This isn't to minimise the abuse I suffered, yet as someone who has gone through a spiritual death and awakening, I know there are many layers to life that we do not initially see. I know when we minimise it is a tactic the ego uses to keep us safe from feeling. But then there comes a time when these tactics begin to harm us rather than help us. They solidify in the body and cause us more pain than the original hurt.

My mother's inability to stand with and for her children felt like the ultimate betrayal and, to a child who couldn't defend herself, it was. To have not taken us away from danger, to have us bow down to wrath was the quickest way to teach someone they have no sovereignty.

I was too young to understand all that went on in my life at the time. Now, having had similar patterns play out in my own life, I see that trauma causes all kinds of maladaptations, and so often we cannot see the wood for the trees. We become locked out of life, unable to fully participate. We freeze, we fawn, we collapse, we blame, we shame, we get stuck. This is not an excuse about causing harm to another or ourselves. Because ultimately all these tactics on some level do. Everything is about our ability to have an expanded awareness so that we can become captains of our own vessels and steer them home to safer shores. And part of that is being able to hold everything with a light touch, with ownership, without judgement, so that we can break the karmic cycles that often plague our family lines.

*

There are consequences to lack of awareness, especially when it affects those we care for. I had to learn to forgive myself and to forgive my mother. I could, because I understood the fear and frozenness that can take place when we have suffered trauma ourselves. The survival mechanisms shroud our hearts and cut off our ability to receive and also give love at any real depth. With awareness comes choice. We realise we do not have to follow our family lineage. We can break the chains. We can change the trajectory of the whole of our ancestral imprints for the generations that came before and for those yet to come.

Our physical genetics run so deep, but not deeper than the lineage of our soul.

I am a believer that we come to learn certain lessons, that we put in motion a set of circumstances that are already preordained for us to experience whilst in this earthly body. Yet how we play them out is up to us. We can choose to do it with love or with harm, but the lessons remain the same.

When we refuse to look at our past, we pass it on through our relationships with our partners, our children, our communities and ourselves. We need to move beyond the pain, blame, shame and guilt. When we don't look at the painful emotions they begin to fester in our being. When we ignore the pain, we invalidate it. We have to see that tending to the pain is prioritising and loving ourselves: we are no longer going to abandon our needs, our truth or our wisdom.

We are all beginning to see just how much we are here to heal our ancestral karma individually, collectively and universally. As you learn how to attune back to your full self, know that your story is yours to tell. It's okay to own how much you have hurt throughout your life. It okay for you to validate your life from your vantage point. You get to love yourself in the way you need to as you learn to re-parent yourself. You get to make choices that are meaningful to you. You get to be the compassionate mother for yourself. You get to let your inner children know, "I've got you", as you learn to navigate yourself out of harm's way.

*

Now I see why a woman like my mother had a child like me. One who, whilst simultaneously drowning in the toxicity of my life, was also able to break free from the stagnating waters and begin to crumble some outworn family patterns. I feel I was born into the perfect circumstances to bring me to the deeper realisations of who I am. Yet, I also feel that our world has been hijacked, infiltrated by a false matrix that makes us believe that disorder is a natural way of being. We have to unravel from all the outdated ways of being that have been passed down our lineage and imprinted in our bones.

We are the containers for much of what our parents have left unattended. It is now time to relinquish so many of the traditions and behaviours that have been handed to us.

But this does not happen without causing pain.

I made many mistakes along the way. I lost family members because of my blind spots and inability and unwillingness to see or feel truth at key times. No one likes to be thought of as a bad mother. Yet in the eyes of one of my daughters this is exactly what I am. As I put pen to paper it will have been almost three years since we last spoke. In her eyes I no longer exist. Our path has similar threads to the journey I took with my own mother. Being raised by a traumatised mother, I myself became a traumatised mother.

I thought that somehow being a mother would solve everything when it came to healing my trauma. That having something – someone – to love would fill the void I felt inside and stop the pain I felt from my childhood. This wasn't a conscious doing. Like so many of the relationships we enter into, I was operating from a place of co-dependency. Motherhood triggered every nerve ending and every wounding I ever possessed. It opened the doorway for my own story to finally be seen by myself and for the deeper healing to occur. Motherhood cracked open the façade I had placed over my childhood wounds in order to survive.

I believe that as souls we come to play roles in each other's lives. My daughter and I walking away from each other was the hardest thing we did. Yet within it was a deeper healing. I could cut the cords between myself and my mother, finally letting her go in full peace. I was able to see from a wider lens the pain I caused by walking away from her. I could see how futile the attempts to make her into something she could never be were. In the cracks of my own split, I could see more light. I could allow more space to open in my system so that I could soften and allow myself to be met by my inner truth with more peace and more acceptance.

My daughter couldn't have played a more perfect role. We were both so embedded in the victim triangle: I was the villain in her life and she in mine. Just as my mother was initially in mine. We were the catalyst that activated our deeper ancestral wounding our lineage carried for centuries, we played mother as martyr, the battered wife and the lost woman interchangeably, each of us connected to the thread of the other.

I appreciate each of these women in my motherline's journeys and acknowledge the legacy of abuse that was passed on through us. I am very proud that this lifetime was the time when I have had the ability to say no and finally put an end to specific family patterns. I knew when I found out I was going to be a grandmother that I did not wish to carry the story of abuse, particularly around sexual wounding, any further. But breaking that karmic cycle came at a cost.

*

When there is the absence of true nourishment in the mothering we receive, we either become over-givers to try and recreate the feeling of lack, or we create scenarios where we constantly feel depleted. We cut ourselves off from life afraid to receive in any way. We see life as something to strive at. We get stuck in poverty thinking, constantly pushing forward in order not to feel or take in life's nectar. Life becomes a battlefield.

For a lot of my life, I struggled to let nourishment or real love in. I would see any form of real love as an attachment. The whole of my nervous system was back to front: to me any type of closeness equalled violation. It made me a magnet for life to come at me in a 'hard knock' way. Life would send lessons to crack me open in order to receive its medicine. It was a very violent yet normalised way to live.

When your father is physically violent and you are strong-willed you learn to become your mother's protector too…and anyone else's that gets caught in the crossfire of their dramas. You become the good girl, the high achiever; you learn to neglect what is truly in your heart. You learn that relationships with men must hurt, and you drift through life wanting to be loved or to love. I became my mother's therapist and confidante, she would tell me of her struggles with her relationship with my father and that kind of emotional offloading can stress the nervous system of a child. Especially if you have been emotionally neglected too and are suffering the consequences of abusive prying hands upon your body. You have no capacity to hold it. It goes deep into the body and gets stuck: a disaster in the making when it comes to autoimmune health.

Eventually the body begins to attack itself. I was often in and out of hospital as a child with severe throat conditions: an outward refection of my inability to speak out about what was happening to me. When your caregivers are overburdened with their own pain and are emotionally bankrupt, then you are ill-equipped to grow into an emotionally balanced adult. This is in no way excusing behaviour, yet it does highlight how patterns of abuse are passed down.

I don't think my mother's needs and desires were ever listened to by anyone, not even herself. She collapsed under the burden of her unlived dreams. Stuck in the wounding of her feminine, she blamed all of life for where she was at. At the height of her manic episodes she would bewail the invisible family curse. She never had anyone she really felt she could rely on and she sabotaged herself all throughout her life. But she couldn't see it.

My mother was a co-dependent. I am saying that with love as I know the realms of co-dependent relationships all too well myself. She never had the volition to leave. She spoke about it often enough, but was unable to muster the strength to do it wholeheartedly. She was from a time when women stood by their man no matter what, and leaving wasn't an option for many. All she knew was that men dominated the home and demanded things be done their way. The paradigm was so deeply invalidating to her feminine ways that she was unable to see herself as a full woman with knowing. My mother, being the woman she was, worked hard to uphold our public image of the happy family.

*

For many years I couldn't take the thought that my life was so traumatic. I minimised it and stuffed it down and made myself think it wasn't as bad as it was. I dissociated. I deluded myself. I detached from the truth and invented a different narrative. Our stories can be too painful to hold. Our hearts close and we slowly shift the story to suit our needs. There are often parts of us that need to numb out because we literally cannot accept the fact that our primal relationships were based on abuse. Especially when it is our mother. I did this for years. As children we often turn it upon ourselves in order to survive and receive the limited nourishment we need. We learn that love comes with distortion: you begin to gaslight yourself to alleviate your confusion. This confusion stretched into my own relationship with my children. I was so wrapped up in my own pain. I became my own mother who couldn't see the abuse happening to her own children at the hands of others.

When you never learnt to take care of yourself, it's hard to understand that your erratic behaviour is because you are filled with your own trauma. When I gave birth no one really gave a second thought about the emotional needs of the mother. That was just the way life was. No one told you how to be a mother. As a young mum there were a lot of painful feelings relating back to my mother. No matter what I worked on – career, money, relationships – things always seemed to come back to her limiting beliefs, the way she had loved and given her power away. It took eleven years after my mother's death for me to finally realise I needed help.

I will never know if my mother knew what was happening to me when I was a child. If she did, she blocked it out because it was too painful to acknowledge. But here is the rub: when we stop ourselves from seeing and feeling the pain of abuse, we begin to lose our ability to stand up and be the fierce mother in action. I can feel that in my own story: the places where I checked out because the truth was too much to take. It was too much to acknowledge that my parents could harm me so violently. Too much to take that out in the world there were others who wished to harm children too. And too much to take that I too could have caused harm. I feel where I relinquished the responsibility of being a mother. I feel the places where the tables were turned on me and I had to become a mother way before my time. I feel the places where I had to mother my mother, and in turn my children, at times, had to mother me. When we burden our children with our emotional pain, everyone suffers. We become women afraid of our emotional landscape, trapped in limited behaviours, unable to stand in our power.

*

No matter how hard my life has been I have always known I was here for something greater than what I was told I was. As a black woman born in England, the story I was told of my life was very limited. Yet as a child who would daydream and look to the stars, I knew I was connected to something far greater. I knew I was here to make waves, to speak a different narrative to the norm which always felt confusing to my feminine soul.

Each time I sit with the notion that my gift at this time to the world is one of carrying the codes of the Mother I have to laugh at the irony. To many an outsider my journey as a mother could be seen to have failed in some way because I am estranged from my eldest daughter. Yet each time I feel that sense of unworthiness or doubt, the Great Mother comes and offers me reassurance that who better to tell Her story than someone who has seen and experienced all sides of it.

Being bumped along the ancestral line, as I witnessed the journey of my youngest daughter becoming a mother and thus transforming me into grandmother, has enabled me to see the bigger picture of how we all play parts in each other's and the collective evolutionary journey of our humanity. The narrative then becomes how we can then recontextualise trauma into a new story, to see it as a doorway to a richer existence. This notion may not be for everyone. Not all are ready or will ever enter here. But this is what the Mother is calling us to do now. It is a journey into navigating the more subtle and contrasting realms of our reality. This is an accumulation of lifetimes of work as we open the narrative wider and learn to expand the holding capacity of our nervous systems: a skill that is more about being with the shattered parts of ourselves, than it is healing them. Acceptance of all our wounded parts is everything.

Taking up the responsibility (the ability to respond) to this calling, I remember that this is my story and my medicine and a living legacy for my lineage. I have the power to recreate myself anew. This is a redemption song of my wild tamed heart. A remembrance of the infinite powers that lie within and our divine right to live freely. It's a story that aims to make sense of a world where women like me give away their power in the name of love, discarding their hopes, dreams and longings in the name of progress, until there is nothing left. A world where women become empty shells, abandoned carcasses devoid of any signs of life.

I have no choice but to dig up the bones of this untold story. My soul demands it.

EXERCISE

THE STORY OF YOUR LIFE

Write out the story of your life. Be as imaginative and factual as you need and want to be. This is your story and your interpretation. Your validation and approval of self. Your chance to express whatever feelings you need to. Writing out your story can bring insight into repetitive patterns and help you to gain a greater perspective.

You don't have to write it from beginning to end like a biography. You can write it out as a play or fairytale to give yourself some distance if you need. Or get creative: draw or paint a picture, model something in clay. Use dance and movement if that calls to you. Let the story emerge as itself – be spontaneous with what arises.

Whatever form you choose, here are some basic guidelines to support you:

- Work in allotted time slots so you give yourself time to process the material that emerges. Don't dwell too long. This can be as detrimental as ignoring your pain.

- You may want to set up a sacred space to honour the process: light a candle, set an intention, focus on your breathing, get centred in your body.

- If deep emotions arise, take time out and be gentle with yourself.

- Slow things right down, bring a sense of inner stillness to the process.

- When finished close the activity – blow out the candle and give yourself time to move back into your daily life.

- Leave the story for a while – take time for it to digest – then revisit it with a new set of eyes: What is it telling you?

- Do you need to express it to another? Be selective who you pick as your witness. You may gain new insights if you ask for reflections on your story.

Dear Woman,

Do you ever sit and ponder just how miraculous you are?

You carry at the centre of your being a portal that bridges time and space.

A portal that births souls.

Breathe that all the way in for a moment.

Let what you have forgotten truly begin to be remembered

So you can sense the awe that comes from your tremendous life-giving powers,

Something that for all too long has gone unrecognised and disowned.

The time of the false matrix is coming to an end.

We are shifting over onto a new grid of life-giving abundance,

A new frequency that recognises the true nature of your being.

The vessel of woman is so needed to hold and anchor it.

Can you allow yourself to feel the magnitude of such a thing?

The Mother

The medicine of the Mother is a gift of love that is here to help us alchemise and digest our collective trauma. She came to me for that very reason during one of my biggest breakdowns and taught me how to love myself again. She descended into and around me like a cloud of pink mist as I chose to leave this world. It was a love like I had never felt before. She stated that the choice to stay or leave was mine and mine alone. There was no judgement, only the explanation that the soul is eternal and I will live on whether this body does or not. If I chose to stay, She declared that She would help me see why my life had turned out the way it had. But if I chose to leave, I would have to go through the lessons again.

In that moment I could see that everything in the universe is of made of Her energy and we are simultaneously weaving and creating this reality with Her. All our experiences, all of our timelines, all of our energetic thought forms and imprints are what are keeping this incredible matrix together. Deep down in our bones we are all imprinted with the spark of life, with a knowing that we are born from something far greater than just our human genetic makeup. We are sparks of the Mother.

*

As a child growing up, I had no mental concept of a feminine aspect of God. I went to church on Sundays and heard only of a loving yet wrathful male presence that, if you pleased him, would spare your soul. And living with an angry father, the punishment of an unseen sky-daddy felt a real possibility. Yet when I looked up to the sky all I felt was love and a sense that everything I was being told was a lie. I hated even then that all the women mentioned from the Bible were seen in some negative way. They were the root of all evil: there was something innately wrong with us. But to me, the things they were calling bad and sinful made me afraid of my own body's functions which continued right up until my mother's death. Her departure was the opening that began to awaken me to the different facets and many layers of the Mother. The longing for Her to return led me down a spiralling path, looking to fill the void and lack of love I felt.

The Great Mother is the force of creation. She creates for creation's sake. She flows through all life. She has always been here, hidden in plain sight. So much so I realised that I had actually ignored her presence throughout my whole life. Even when, after my mother's death in 2008 and later that of my partner in 2015, She entered as the Dark Mother and began to dismantle my life in order to help me connect to the deeper truth of me, I fought Her all the way. But in doing so I was only fighting aspects of myself, because we are birthed through Her when we come to this realm. We are held in the void of the Mother, Her Cosmic Womb.

In their book *The Cosmic Mother*, Monica Sjöö and Barbara Mor describe the Cosmic Mother as the regenerative and birthing force of the universe. This is how I feel Her too, as the generative force from which all aspects of life spring forth through the darkness of the Comic Womb. The Great Mother carries facets of all aspects of the feminine: the warrior, the maiden, crone, benevolent mother, the dark Mother, the queen, the goddess etc. She seeds all and has done so from the beginning of time. She sends forth these aspects so that each of us can relate to the flavour of Her that most suits our genetic make-up so all facets of Her can be out in the world. So that each of us can begin to open to Her, She will come to us in a form we can recognise. Each of us is a fractal of the whole. What part of Her calls you now?

I believe that because my life was so dark in its formation, I found it hard to accept Her love, just as I did with earthly love. The only way I could begin to let Her in was when She first came as the Dark Mother.

The dark of the Mother assists us in unleashing our power and gifts through the process death and rebirth. She helps remove all distortions and limiting beliefs about yourself and life. She breeds courage in your bones to be able to face your darkness and shadows. She shows you the beauty of being stripped naked. She teaches what it means to back yourself. She shows you there is nothing to fear from being in the dark without a clear sense of direction, because ultimately She shows you how to navigate the dark and soak up the nourishment from the earth.

The Cosmic Mother is the primordial blackness, the feminine essence that births all things…as well as having the power to take life too. We shy away from the death part of her cycle but it is an essential part of life. The dark is our ally.

The force of the Mother cannot be found through the mind, She is connected to us through our felt experience. You cannot find her through action or consumption, instead we come into contact with Her through stillness and through the body. To know Her is to feel. Her signature frequency is so different from the false matrix we have created here on Earth that feels like it is fundamentally anti-life. We feel the difference in our hearts and minds and the impactful effect on our nervous systems when we attune with Her.

Being incubated in Her blackness is an important aspect of our awakening process. All life is birthed from the dark. Through it we expand back into the vastness of all that is, into the nothingness, back into the blackness of Her great Void, where all life springs forth. We come back renewed and cleansed.

Nurturing and grounding, Her energy brings us into a state of receptivity and flow. Her aim is to always bring things back into alignment, even if that means dismantling your life. In a world that is out of balance, Her force can feel chaotic as She weaves Her way back into this reality as a force for our evolution. She is the force of creation Herself. Like thick molasses or a swift disruptive storm, Her power is wielded to bring life back into harmonic balance. And though Her presence may initially feel like disruption, She ultimately feels like home. She is the realm of the love that we have all been searching for.

Her transmission of love is like an umbilical cord that penetrates up through the earth and draws us into the blackness of her womb. Mother, is Matter, is Ma. Matter comes from the same Latin root as the word mother. Right now we are manifesting Her essence into matter.

EXERCISE

MEDITATION

Sit or lie quietly and invite the Great Mother to hold you from behind. Let Her presence embrace you, feel Her unconditional love wrapping around you. Invite in your inner child/children and hold them in your arms. Whatever age comes up is the one/s that need to feel the love in that moment. Caress them and send them loving thoughts, as the Mother simultaneously does that to you. Feel Her love penetrating through you and through to your child/children. Know that Her love is always available to you. You will know it when you feel it. It is unlike any love you will have felt before.

(If this feels too confronting, an alternative is to lie or stand on the earth and imagine Mother Earth holding and healing you that way.)

The Mother Codes

Our bodies are living libraries. We carry codes of consciousness within them. Our blood is filled with the stories of our ancestors.

The current frequencies of the Mother that are coming through to assist humanity within this evolutionary period of growth are calling for a network of bodies to bring them through. Like the structures of nature, the mycelium of mushrooms or root systems of the trees, they need us all to play our part. It is too much for one person to hold and bring them through to this realm. We are not doing this alone.

Nor do we need to go anywhere to seek the Mother. Her codes are imprinted in us by the sheer fact that we are alive. You can think of Her codes like an energy or frequency that is encoded in your DNA. Just like physical traits, we have information codes that we each carry and attune to. Like the seed of the oak tree, the acorn, holds the genetic codes that spell out how the tree will grow. Our soul is the same. We hold coding about who we are to become, the gifts we carry and brought into this lifetime with us.

This innate wisdom is buried deep inside you, passed down your lineage. It has lain there silent, dormant, waiting for activation by words or an image or a feeling, which, like a key, unlocks the information that resides in your body. A bit like a radio transmitter signal going out to be received or the downloading of a computer file. We can think of our psyche, brain and body as the software we are rewriting with the original coding we hold in the blueprint of our cells. We are clearing out the toxic limiting beliefs we have had passed down to us through generations, the prescribed programme set out by society. Our bodies truly have kept the score and now it is ready for a reboot as we say "no!".

Codes are felt on an energetic level and we can attune our sensitivity to pick these up and transmit them to one another. You can get a sense of what I mean when I speak to the phenomenon that happens when groups gather in meditation practice and begin to feel the same thing and use that collective energy to shift and change the environment around them or influence someone's healing.

We are learning to decipher Her coding and translate it into a language we can understand. Her wisdom, more often than not, comes in poetic language to bypass the mind. This is especially true when the path you embody is based around oracular transmission. The codes that are landing at this time to assist the evolution of humanity are asking for those that hear or feel their presence to do our best to interpret them and put them into words so that others may begin to feel the truth of what is being asked to be birthed at this time of our grand awakening.

As the feminine rises, we are reclaiming not only in word but in power the names we have been taught to fear: witch, mystic, priestess, seer… We can reclaim these aspects of self and see the wisdom we hold by embracing the fullness of the paths She is asking us to take. We then become the wisdom-keepers of this realm. We are reclaiming the medicine held deep down in our bones. We see that in doing so we have the ability to change our consciousness and the environment around us as we loosen the grip of patriarchal rule.

....

MY STORY

I hold the codes of the Mother in me. I am here to be a transmission for them. Throughout my life there have been many times when the force of the feminine has been calling to rise through me, yet I didn't know what it was at the time. Way before I even knew anything about spirituality, a psychiatrist recommended yoga for stress. During my first term, as my body began to relax into the flow of the postures, I felt a ripple of what I now know to be the force of shakti, the feminine, moving through my body. It came in the form of orgasmic waves. These unfamiliar sensations put me off doing the practice for a while. It felt too foreign to my being. Too out of range for someone like me, who at the time didn't want to feel anything and used alcohol to numb out. I decided to switch tactics and moved onto meditation. Nothing could happen here without movement, right?

How wrong could I have been! The Mother is persistent when She wants to get your attention: She will never stop nudging you awake. Four sessions in, I went into a trance-like state and my body began to move of its own accord in spiral motions. Suffice to say, whatever this mysterious force was, it was going to find a way to move through me whether I wanted it to or not.

I was called naïve or idealistic all my life. A daydreamer who wanted things to be beautiful and not dark like they were. Now I know it was because I always had a thread connected to a parallel reality where life was truly in alignment with the Mother and the natural world. And now that knowing is beginning to flourish as I hold that vision for humanity. I am here to assist in bringing in a reality we have been conditioned to forget. This book is the beginning of planting more seeds in relation to that.

It is a reality that emanates from the realm of the Mother: the Mother World[*]. One that puts the natural world at the forefront. A world where we are all tended to, nourished, honoured and we get to feel how sacred we are.

I hold the codes of the Mother and her world deep within. I feel the codes of

---

[*] I first came across the term the Mother World when invited to partake in the first in a series of summits called Return to the Mother World curated and created by Emmi Mutale. You can find out more about the Mother World Summit and book of the same name at returntothemotherworld.com The term the Mother World is one that is becoming prevalent in the field of feminine wisdom as more of us hear Her call to rise.

the Original Woman[*], not as fantasy but as truth. My passion is that of deep connection, my gift to ignite erotic innocence with precision, my contribution to elevate, illuminate and celebrate the sacred, to leave the world and my life in a better way than I found it. This is who I am: I cannot be any other way. I did not choose this path, it chose me. Are you here to remember that you came here for that too?

....

EXERCISE

CONNECTING TO OUR ANCESTORS

We can call on the help of our benevolent ancestors as we reconnect with the Mother codes. They need to be asked. They will not interfere with our free will. In our asking we are honouring their presence and their wisdom. We are surrendering to their knowing as we take a stance of deep listening. Caroline Seckinger, when talking about her deep ancestral creative work, says that we don't need an elaborate ritual to work with our ancestors.[†] We can simply begin by acknowledging that they are there. We can state our intention as to why we are making contact. We can light a candle in their honour as a regular occurrence to let them know we are there too. Say a daily prayer, give thanks and gratitude for the unseen world. Give thanks for the body you are in and that you are able to be a conduit between this world and theirs. Bring them an offering, something for them to receive and use as a conduit to convey their offerings back to you in this physical realm. Speak to them, even if you do not know them by name. Know you are building a relationship between you. Don't just do this when you need them: this is a two-way relationship and needs some nurturing on your part.

---

[*] The term Original Woman was first brought to my awareness via Diane Beaulieu and her contribution to the previously mentioned Mother World Summit. She spoke of a time when women could walk the earth uninhibited. I had an instantaneous activation into a deep remembrance of this time. This is the way of feminine wisdom. You can find out more about Diane's work at sacredwomanawakening.com

[†] Caroline Seckinger, founder of 'Her Eternal Ceremonial Knives,' has beautiful tools, a connection ritual and altar cloth designed to help you connect with your ancestral linage at carolineseckinger.com

Our ancestors love to make their presence known. As I wrote that very line a butterfly flew to my window. This is very unusual as it is the middle of winter here in the UK. The butterfly was a symbol that represented my mother. I wore her butterfly brooch at her funeral. To me it is a sign she is listening and always around.

We can use our imagination to reconnect to the imprint of the Original Woman. Can you allow yourself to open to the prospect that you had a female ancestor somewhere down the line who was safe to walk the world in her fullness? Can you allow yourself to feel that as a true cellular memory? Or maybe you see this imprint as a lifetime you have lived yourself. Can you let it circulate in the cauldron of your womb as you bring more substance to your musings? Let the power of creation move through you. Make room for it to grow. Let the seed of it expand through your whole being. Imagine her growing in size and life and standing before you. What would you ask her to show you? What wisdom would you ask her to share?

Invite her wisdom deeper into you. Give thanks that you are part of a network of women waking to this deeper truth, that they too carry the codes of the Original Woman and are bringing them forward as a gift for humanity. So much knowing can come through the portal of our wombs when we ask to be connected to the web of universal wisdom. You know you are not doing this alone. You feel the presence of our foremothers. We remember how our cells are part of the Mother, how they are part of the Earth and that we are one and the same. Generation upon generation has travelled this path.

....

The Mother Wound

Our disconnect from the Mother turned us into rootless orphans, and created a wound so great it rippled down our lineages until now, when we have collectively agreed to heal the mother wounds. Bethany Webster in her work on the mother wound describes it as a social condition rooted in patriarchy which exists on four levels: personal, cultural, spiritual and planetary. In her book *Discovering the*

Inner Mother, she names a set of beliefs that have a devastating impact on our lives, from which distinct behaviours arise that disrupt the relationship between mother and daughter; devalue women and their place in the world; keep us disconnected from a higher power and life itself; and ultimately drive us to destroy the Earth and bring with it a threat to all life.

We do not need to be in contact with our mother to heal this wound, in fact she doesn't not even need to be alive (as in my case). To ignore this wound has a ripple effect of untapped potential that stretches down through the generation and keeps us playing out limiting patterns and beliefs.

Our conflicted relationships with our mothers need to be embraced so that we can finally begin to heal this wound in a bigger collective way. Around the time that I began to have growing resentment towards my mother, I couldn't understand why she put up with what she did. I couldn't understand why, like me, she didn't initiate that fire inside. I didn't understand it…until I did. When, in my late twenties, I myself fell into my first dysfunctional relationship, I realised it wasn't an either-or situation: so many factors were at play. The mother wound affects us individually and collectively in so many ways. Its impact goes deep.

The mother wound often plays havoc under the surface of our lives, it seeps into all areas through the cracks created by trauma, which, if not tended to, become gaping holes. It is up to us to shore up those holes and fill the cracks so that we feel whole. Like the Japanese art of repairing broken pottery – *kintsugi* – we repair the cracks and create something more beautiful than was there before. When we tend to the deeper work, when we hold ourselves with compassion and tenderness, when we dare to look at the shadows, we get to bring life back to our numbed parts. We get to touch the blueprint of our being in a way that impacts not only ourselves, but those that came before us and those that will come after us.

According to Webster, some of the ways the mother wound impacts our life when we avoid it are:

- We constantly carry a persistent vague sense that there is something wrong with us.
- We never actualise our potential out of fear of failure or disapproval.
- We have weak boundaries and an unclear sense of self.
- We feel unworthy of creating what we truly desire.

- We never feel safe enough to take up space and voice our truth.
- We arrange our lives around 'not rocking the boat'.
- We self-sabotage when we get close to a breakthrough.
- We unconsciously wait for our mother's permission or approval before claiming our own lives.

This is a pivotal part of our collective story. We each represent a line of women that goes back to the beginning of time, that connects us to the original imprints of the Great Mother and the Original Woman. Our work at this current time is to assist in the rising of the feminine on the planet. We stand shoulder to shoulder with the mothers and grandmothers that came before us. Those that laid the groundwork for us to shift these outdated patterns in this lifetime. Each had a part to play, each a fractal of our Herstory.

We are in a time when our collective mother wound is ripe for healing. Our mothering, our lack of mothering, our insecurities and our greatness are all on the table as we lean into what is real and true. The Mother can give us what our human mothers could not. To let the Mother in fully we must dismantle the prisons we have built for ourselves to keep ourselves in a false sense of safety. It is only then that we are able to show up in our true soul essence. To be in the flow of creation from moment to moment we need to soften. We learn to be vulnerable and embrace our perfectly raw messy selves.

The journey to reconnect to my body and people and to the Earth has been long and arduous at times. Yet I persevered because of the turmoil I know trauma leaves behind when not tended to. Plus, I see a part of our role whilst being here on Earth is to leave our ancestry in a better way than when we were birthed into it. We are here to honour our ancestors as well as grow from our life experiences. I see women healing their wounding as an essential component at this time of our Herstory. We need women in every sector of society who have the capacity to say no to the growing turbulence as we dismantle all the messages from society that have dishonoured what it is to be a mother and/or a woman. Messages that taught us to distrust our bodies and observation skills, and ultimately our intuition. Messages that made our intrinsic nature a pathology. We were seen as weak for being our beautiful emotional selves. And for a time in our history women were locked away in mental institutions just for being misunderstood in their womanhood.

When we tend to the mother wound, we clear the way for our authentic nature to come online, and we begin to be disruptors of the current systems just through our embodiment. We then get to build and create systems that actual work for us. Systems that can transform communities and support everyone in them. We get to feel empowered to make the changes necessary.

If we do not heal down our lineages, we will see more of what we see today. And in my honest opinion I feel we have gone way too far down the line in a misaligned direction when it comes to the suppression of feminine ways. We see before us the distortion that happens when She is left out of the picture. We end up with systems that are inverted and inorganic. What we really want is a balance of both the masculine and feminine principles, in order to get there we have to heal the mother wound first.

Healing the mother wound is not about blaming our mother, but embracing the wisdom we glean from the relationship we had, whether good or bad. If we look at ourselves through compassionate eyes, we come to understand how things can change for the better. We get to hold each other tenderly so the true healing can begin. And yes, it takes courage to lay it all out there. I often have a vulnerability hangover when being transparent about my past. Yet I continue because I have seen the miraculous transformation within self and others that can occur when we bring our skeletons out of the closet to be held with reverence rather than shame.

When we begin to journey with the mother wound there is a natural separation that takes place as we begin to see our mothers as their individual selves and in their fragile human nature. We get to see their flaws as well as their gifts, and we get to forgive and accept them for who they truly are, beyond what we needed them to be.

Becoming our own mother is the ultimate goal through all of this, as well as being able to feel into a greater motherly force and presence that is always loving and supporting us, even when it hurts. Our mothers birthed us into the world and brought us life. The path we walk is ours and ours for a reason. We have to remember that our matriarchal DNA has been passed from womb to womb through our motherline since the first woman. And it is this key piece of information that awakens the remembrance through space and time of what is rising to be met at this time in humanity's history.

MY STORY

What if, as part of your healing journey, you have to release a family member or your work? I know that uncomfortable truth. Sometimes standing in our vulnerable truth means releasing obligations, especially when showing the truth of who you are means those close to you may reject you for doing so. They have a choice to either be in connection or disconnect if it is too confronting. They may be activated in your presence.

As a mother I was activated in my eldest child's presence, just as she was in mine. It was the same with my mother and I. We rubbed up against each other's smallness and bigness in a way that created nothing but friction. What we brought out in each other when we brought the full version of ourselves out was not good. We were unable to give one another the permission to be fully sovereign beings. In service to one another we had to step away to begin the healing of the generational line.

This went against everything I had been taught: that you must not fall out of line with your family. When we have to see the people around us because of family events and occasions it can be hard. We have to keep coming back to the vulnerable truth that the relationship was for a season and not a lifetime; that beyond our roles we are incompatible. We begin to see that soul lineage and family lineage are two different things. The mother wound can sometimes mean that we have to break the chain first, before reunification can take place.

EXERCISE

CLEARING THE DISTORTED PATTERNS OF MOTHERHOOD

Our words are incantations and hold power. We can command with our words, breaking patterns passed down through our lineage. We have the capability to break the chain and bring in a new way of being. Use the following statements[*] as a guide. Feel free to add your own and make this your practice.

Know that when we speak to our bodies they respond. With each statement feel what sensations arise. It is always seeking release. Each time you speak these statements, repeating the exercise, you begin to build trust between you and your body as you tune in and listen. Know that this isn't about being logical, it's about learning to let the body lead. It knows exactly what it needs to do. You may cry, you may shake. Let the sensation move though you: it is looking for completion.

- I ask that any guilt or shame passed on through my mother that was imprinted in me be released.
- I let go of the judgements of the past. I no longer have to carry them in my being.
- I no longer have to carry the wounds of the previous generations.
- I am perfect, whole and complete just the way I am.
- I release the obligations passed on to me by previous generations that I did not agree to take on.
- I hold the power within me to alchemise all that needs to be. My vessel is an alchemical container.
- I have universal wisdom contained within my cells.
- I have the power to activate my cells into absorbing all the love of the Mother needed to heal the wounding I received as a child.

---

[*] Although this exercise is fully my own, the statements used have been influenced by my time as a student of Perri Chase (for which I am truly grateful), in particular the attendance of her Portal: Mother – a shamanic experiential journey. As I come to complete the writing of this book, I am no longer a student of hers or affiliated with her work.

- I let my being surrender to the wisdom I hold in my body so that I can locate the gifts I hold inside.
- I allow my body to open so that life can move through me and fill my being with the frequency of harmony.
- I no longer have to stay closed down, or think I have to do it all alone. I have the support of life.
- I have the support of the Mother and I feel Her love and nourishment as I learn to receive and release what no longer serves.
- I am enveloped in Her energy and I am safe.
- I ask that all judgements I hold about my mother be released in love.
- I ask that any expectations I have that I will be like my mother be released.
- I see my mother and myself as two separate beings on our own unique paths.
- I release any obligations I still carry that state I had to carry her mistakes.
- I release the obligations that I have to mother my mother.
- I release the story that to be a mother I have to sacrifice or lose myself.
- I release the need for my mother to be perfect.
- I release the idea that I have to be liked in all that I do.
- I release the idea that I am a bad mother.
- I release any resentment I hold because I was not taught how to care for or mother myself.
- I ask that I gain the full feeling of what it means to feel nourished and cared for.
- I ask that the highest version of what Mothering is to be awakened in me
- I release all blame of my mother and of being a mother.
- I release the idea that being a mother means putting myself last and that I have to give up who I am.
- I ask for the full knowing of how to be with my mother in a way that is good for us both.
- I release the belief that I cannot forgive myself.

- I receive the knowing of how to forgive myself and others.
- I forgive myself for who I have been as a mother.
- I release any trauma bonding with my mother and know that it is okay to set boundaries. I am still safe and loved if I do.
- I release any belief or wounding that I was a burden, a mistake or that I was an inconvenience.

Add any other beliefs you feel you would like to release and be lifted.

See the energy of these statements reverberating up and down your ancestral lineage. See a light sending this healing balm to them too. Know that you have the power to shift things just with your voice and intention. You are the keeper of your own destiny.

As things begin to shift state:

"I ask that these limiting beliefs, patterns, or imprints be released from all aspects of my physical, mental, emotional, etherical, energetic, spiritual, auric and universal energy fields across all timelines, realms and dimensions of reality."

State your gratitude (gratitude is a neutralising balm).

As things start to shift, emotions may arise, you may feel tingling in the body, you may yawn, burp, cry, shake or sigh as energy shifts. As the energy begins to settle ask that:

"All aspects of myself that may have been trapped in these limited patterns be returned cleaned at 100% capacity, vibrancy and vitality and the frequencies of my mind, body and soul be revived to full operational capability."

See yourself fill up with your own energies, regenerated and rejuvenated so you can sustain the highest version of yourself. As you continue to fill up with your own energy and light say the following:

"I give thanks that all soul fragments that belong to me are returned back to me, cleansed and renewed. And that all soul fragments that do not belong to me be cleansed with light and returned to whom they belong. I command that all parties involved be brought back to their centre and the boundaries between each of us be strengthened to build healthy nourishing relationships and connections. And so it is!"

Shine your light and let it nourish all those you come into contact with.

....

Welcoming Back the Mother

We are learning to hold ourselves in the state of expansion as more of the Mother's energies come up through and onto the planet in order to guide us. She is calling us to bear witness to our deeper longing. Through Her we learn to face the truth of who we are; to give ourselves permission to show up as our fullest selves, unbridled. You are needed. There will be no turning back once you heed Her call and you will need your wits about you, for you have been in limbo for way too long. You did not choose this path, it chose you. And it will not stop bringing you to attention until you sit up and listen.

When we fully tune into the vibrational frequency of the Mother it has a weightiness to it that roots us into the depth of our being. We see the remembrance of this in the ancient tombs and temples, in the full-bodied form of the goddess. The Venus of Willendorf is a prime example. In our world of distorted masculine values, we have emaciated the feminine. We have slimmed her down, squeezed her ripe juiciness out, left ourselves hungry and thirsting for Her. We embrace the masculine principle of pushing and forcing, devoid of the feminine flow, the body has become our enemy. Mother, is Matter, is Ma. We cannot fully be Her without our embodied being.

Our individual journeys ultimately take us on a path to discover our uniqueness, to uncover our soul gifts and how to offer them to the world. We are living in a time when it is vital that we begin to remember our sacred foundation to be in service to Her ways.

Now is the time. Not just for me but for others too, that are here to resurrect the codes of the Mother. So much of our life is created through the unseen, yet we negate it precisely because it is not seen. Within our cellular memory we have access to the gift of our ancestors and their wisdom across eons of time. We also have deep wisdom we can access that is held in the fabric of the Earth. These memories are waiting for us to tap into and reclaim them. Like time capsules they are held so that we can resurrect the remembrance of the Mother World: a world that is here to restore the vital matrix of life. It is now time to tap into this energy so we can reconnect to this essential essence of life: these are the codes resurrecting.

We have the ability to shift the energetic imprints we sense our souls have come to rectify. We have the capacity to heal up and down the ancestral line.

This is a quantum field of reality and we have the opportunity to play out an infinite number of possibilities. Every choice we make is a new timeline created. As souls we come to play roles in each other's lives. Sometimes those roles are not easy ones. I know the relationship between mother and daughter can be one of the most challenging and also rewarding ones in our lives. This was definitely the case in my experience. Yet there comes a time on our personal journeys when we have to realise that we have to separate from the collective wounding story of mother and tap into the true frequency of Mother.

I know I could not have faced so much of my past without the holding of the Mother. She awakened me to the possibility that my transformation could be tender. That I could stop beating myself up. That I could be a woman who learns to be gentle with herself and with others in my life, especially close intimate relationships. With family and friends I initially had to let go of, now we are finding mutual love for one another and our differences. This understanding can foster a world where we love one another in our painful places. We get to be rooted in our motherly arts from an integrated space of pelvic power and heart, shifting the tide of trauma to lessen humanity's karmic burden.

*

I am…you are…remembering that we are here to bring a transmission of the Mother's love. You carried this knowing as a burden, because you tried to fit in. You held yourself down for so long. But now you no longer resonate with those that can't hear your soul song. Many of those who you have called family, you've had to let them go. You know you came for other things. You came to honour the magic that sits deep in your bones, to free yourself from slavery.

As we awaken from our collective slumber, as we move through this earthly dark night of the soul, Her majestic flow pulses through the dark damp earth to us, through us. As She rises to meet us, She helps us to unravel and discard all that no longer serves. If you feel the resonance of these words, may it activate a remembrance of the purifying essence of Her original creative frequency that is restorative and here to support organic life. Our bodies are the living libraries, the transmitters and receivers of Her frequency.

Call upon the Mother to aid you in your quest to unearth your deeper knowing. Nothing comes with ease until we put Her at the forefront of all that we do. Her call is the strongest magnetic pull you will ever feel. She will stop at nothing to illuminate and awaken you to live your fullest life. Once we are united with Her, we are united with life. She flows through all life. Her love knows no limits and has no bounds; it is timeless. Her devotion to you runs deep. It is always mutual. She flows through you as you flow through Her.

But in order to flow through you, first She has to find a way in.

Dear Woman,

Your true feminine power is your ability to surrender into life,

To open, to receive. To feel the call of your shadows that are asking to be seen.

These are places where you had to abandon yourself in order to survive.

Do not be afraid of the rising darkness within or without.

In embracing them we are all brought the exact medicine we need individually and collectively.

These parts are asking to be held. To be alchemised.

To shift. To be transformed.

To be loved.

Let the darkness be an endless fuel for your own growing power.

PART TWO

RAW

Dear Woman,

Come rest in the darkness of my Cosmic Womb,

Surrender into my healing waters.

Do not be afraid of their watery depths,

For deep in the dark, under the jostling waves of your life

You will find peace here.

Held in the arms of the Mother,

Nestled in a blanket of Her deep nourishing dark earth.

Like a seed She imprints and activates in you an awakening.

You remember that within you is already your fullest potential.

So, take solace as you root down into Her.

She is unlimited in Her giving and you will always be fed

As She guides you to all the places where you have hidden your magic.

Surrender

First you have to relinquish who you were.
 You have to find your way into the darkness,
 And find Her at the heart of it.
 First you have to die to yourself.
 The roadmap to Her is one of surrender.

The Mother will sweep through your life and remove all obstacles to your deeper truth. She teaches you how to be humble and surrender to the path of your calling, to take it seriously and to own it with all of your heart. She calls you to ignite every cell of your being to put down your sword and surrender to Her will. She invites you to enter into a state of deep surrender so you can reside in her realm and let the process of undoing begin. The depth of the feminine can only be known by our undoing. Through the unravelling of constraints that confine us. The Mother comes to shake loose all falsehoods that bind us.

It can be tempting to want to shut down when the winds of change roll in. Our human self may not like this, but our soul understands it. To move through this, we have to be reborn. It took a near death experience for me to acknowledge the truth of that. For you, it may be loss in another way. But you do not have to blow up your life to transform. We can learn to be held when our lives begin to rearrange. We can learn to hold our centre in the eye of the storm.

Change can be terrifying, I know that. With real change, a part of our old identity must die. We must let it. Or it will destroy us. Surrender is the dropping of all the barriers we have created as mechanisms of safety around our wounds. In surrender we shift tracks from trying to do it all alone, to being in faith that we will be caught when we take a leap towards the call. Ask yourself what would happen if you let Her hold you so Her transformational force can carve you into a being that is led by soul. To be fully present in the body we must face the things we have pushed into the recesses, deep into the tissues, stored in the flesh of our beings. We learn that strength comes in the shape of softness, in opening to what is present. Allowing ourselves to become still enough to hear what is calling us forth. The voice of the soul is subtle. The voice of the Mother can be too.

The path to Her will often lead you in a way that makes you feel that you are going around in circles. Just as in a labyrinth or a spiral, we move in a way that isn't linear. Our role in the process is to be in a state of surrender. We are remembering we can see in the dark and that it is our ally as we trust in the Mother and ourselves once again.

In a world that has us focusing outwardly on all that is fast and bright, we can be afraid of the stillness and the dark. We fill our lives with activity, forever searching for answers to find purpose and meaning that we will never find without going inward. Stillness doesn't necessarily mean inactivity. It is an active process, a balance between doing and being. Just like the land, we need fallow time to replenish and go into deeper enquiry. When we lack real space and time for this vital process, we can become irritable, frustrated and exhausted.

When we allow ourselves some stillness in our lives, we can begin to create the appropriate internal space to also appreciate how far we have come in our lives and celebrate our achievements. Celebration is a vital component of the process of surrender. We need to acknowledge where we are on the path. We have to consciously enter into a period of stillness so we can hear the more subtle whispers calling us forth to deeper change. Somewhere inside us we know that stillness brings all the sediment of our forgotten desires to the surface.

EXERCISE

PERMISSION TO BE STILL

Your path doesn't have to be as extreme as mine was. You can find your path in much more gentle way. You can begin the process by finding pockets of stillness in your life so that you can feel what is asking for your presence. Even beginning with 10-20 minutes a day, bring your energy and awareness to rest into the back of the body and ask a question about your path. This simple step will start the process of reconnecting and opening up to your internal world, which is the gateway into the realm of the Mother World. See what arises as you set an intention to attune to your internal frequency.

I recommend that you create a day of honouring and ritual where you get to know to yourself on a deeper level through reflection and contemplation.

- What arises in you at the thought of that? Is it fear, a feeling of being selfish or a full-blown yes?

- Even this single question is a start to see where you can and can't give to yourself. It tells you so much about your relationship to spaciousness and stillness in your life.
- How might you get 24 hours totally to yourself? Can you book or borrow somewhere away from your normal environment in a quiet area?
- Or, if you stay at home, can you set some boundaries around carving out time for yourself? Communicate clearly to those around you so you are not disturbed.
- Set an intention – what do you wish to discover from this time alone?
- Create a sacred space to honour yourself – light a candle as a symbol of opening the space or draw a circle around it to mark the start of the process.
- After this, the idea is not to plan but to go with the flow and see what wants to be revealed in the moment.
- At the end of the time mark the end of the process with a simple ritual – close the circle, thank yourself and the space.
- Note your dreams if possible during this time – write down your insights.
- Give yourself readjustment time, especially if things were revealed to you that were surprising.
- If you feel it is right, share your reflections on this experience with a trusted person. Often when we are witnessed or receive constructive reflections then more insights are revealed.
- Are you able to give yourself more than 24 hours? Vipassana meditation – the practice of noble silence – is a practice conducted over a multi-day silent retreat. No phones, no pen or paper, no talking, no eye contact with other participants. Just you and you alone – it could be something you plan down the line.

....

Learning to let down the guard around the heart is a process of decalcification. For someone like me who has seen so much tragedy, I had a choice to either become more hardened and closed or to feel the pain and soften and open. It takes courage to go against the grain in a fast-paced world that constantly tells us we have to harden to survive. It takes courage to take down our defences and let ourselves be fully seen. To let the true self shine through, to open ourselves to vulnerability. To surrender can feel disorientating. When opening our hearts we have to learn to be gentle with ourselves. As we learn to surrender, we allow the presence of the Mother to hold us as we learn to hold ourselves.

It takes a conscious choice to start opening up to the unfolding path before us. When we start to move through life with a less guarded heart, when we speak from our vulnerability, we bring in a softness so needed at this time, that differs from the harsh reality we have collectively created. When we bury grief, we create war inside us. And war outside us. Opening the heart allows us to heal our deep separation from the Mother that has caused imbalance in the world.

The Descent

Dying to the old is an essential part of surrendering to life. Yet as a species we have become afraid of this part of the process. We vilify instead of normalising the fact that death and darkness are a part of the whole. We have become afraid to feel, afraid to descend into the unknown. We live in a world that wants to medicate the darkness rather than gain the medicine from it. This is why it can take a long time to move through the darkness: we are taught to hide our pain, to push through our grief, to have a hatred for our undoing. We can go willingly into the dark or get dragged into it. When we don't listen to the cues life sends our way to stop and surrender and move in a new direction, we can make the descent more difficult than it actually is.

The inward journey to make contact with the Mother World shares many of the features of the ancient myths of the descent to the underworld like those from the stories of Inanna and Persephone. Both paths require acts of surrender and dying to the old. Both ask us to leave the known and familiar and enter into a cycle of death and rebirth. This is familiar to us from the natural world. In winter, life slows down and goes inwards, just as in this process of surrender to the Mother World we too have to embrace slowing down. The descent can be different each time and, just like the cycles of life, we move through those cycles over and over again. The realm of the Mother World is a place that in its darkness holds a lot of light. Her realm feels like being buried, like a seed in rich fertile soil. We then get to see and feel the nourishment of being in the dark.

We begin to understand that there is nothing to fear and in fact the dark is a place that holds a lot of compassionate energy for our pain and for our potential growth. Yet once we enter into Her realm there is no bargaining with Her, for we have entered into an agreement to find truth, no matter how uncomfortable that may be to our personalities. What we excavate from this place then becomes gold for our growth as we alchemise our pain into power.

MY STORY

Our calling isn't always straight forward or clear. It may be attached to the very thing you are running from like I was. It may be the very thing you have the most work to clear up distorted patterns around or the most heartache you have to feel. You may never want to answer the call. Surrendering to the call of the Mother has not been easy for me. There have been times when I have questioned as to whether this was truly my path because along the way I have been asked to give up many things I thought were aligned with my purpose.

Twice in my life I have been asked by a call from the Mother to let go of my business. Both times I was at a point when I was just getting into the groove and enjoying my work. Both times I heard an internal voice that was so to the point – *"This will be your last client"*; *"This will be the last course you run"*. Both made no logical sense. The first time was a definite call into the underworld on a trajectory that I have since been told followed the descent of Inanna;[*] a path I traversed with little or no guidance. When I came out the other side, I tried to put myself back into my old life. Of course that didn't work. Within a couple of years, I was dragged back under into the realm of the Mother, a completely unknown realm to me at the time. One where death took on a new form: one of stillness and quiet.

---

[*] When I first went into the dark, I spoke to friends who each gave me pieces of the puzzle. When I described the figure that spoke to me, they remarked that it sounds like the Dark Goddess. On researching what that could mean I came across a book called *Journey to the Dark Goddess – How to Return to your Soul* by Jane Meredith (2012), within which she describes the descent of Inanna. It was a confirmation that something bigger was happening to me than I had any previous awareness of.

Dear Woman,

You have been taught to become a mere shadow of yourself.

To forget that without you, there is no life.

No us. No being. Nobody.

Do you ever sit and feel the pulse of life that throbs inside of you?

Do you tune into the cyclical nature of your being?

A micro version of the macro Universal Womb where all life originated.

Do you give thanks that your vessel is a doorway to that very cosmic force?

Do you feel the part you are here to play in reviving this ancient narrative?

If you do anything for yourself and for humanity today,

Place your hands on your belly and give thanks for what you hold inside you,

For the tide of the in and out breath of life that you mirror on its behalf.

Can you allow yourself to come into true alignment with that?

Navigating the Shadow

We have to start reframing how we view the dark and the shadow. There is a paradigm within the realms of patriarchal spirituality that speaks only of ascension, stating that we must solely embrace that which is love and light. This is utterly dangerous as it views living within the full human experience as somehow lacking virtue. All the while, the piles of unexpressed feelings lie rotting, swept under carpets, hidden from sight. We can no longer turn our heads only to the sky and forget why we came here in the first place, to be fully embodied. I say this with conviction because I was a person who thought the only solution to my pain was to not feel my pain. That acting as if everything was okay, would make everything okay. I know different now. The shadowy parts of us that are seeking integration will always knock at the door.

The shadow is all that we put in the dark, sometimes consciously, but mostly unconsciously – we hide things there, thinking they are not the truth of who we are. But in reality, they are truer than the projected image we present. Often, they are our deepest and truest desires. The things we have been told to hide about ourselves. The things that we were told to feel shameful about. So much of our energy gets lost ignoring the shadow, yet ultimately it is the place that holds our greatest gifts. The things we place in the shadow are often the parts of us that were deemed too big or bold by another. Too much, too different, too out of the other's range of understanding so we were forced to hide them, place them in the shadows and turn against ourselves because we held onto the message that there was something defective with that part of who we are.

Once we can begin to acknowledge the parts of ourselves we have put in the shadow and take responsibility for and accept them, then the shadow can begin to be our greatest ally instead of our biggest fear. We begin to see that the dark is the place where all new life begins, whether that is a seed in the ground or a baby in the womb or an idea born out of abstract thought from the void. We have to learn to love the shadow because ultimately it is the most tender part of us. The part that holds the greatest potential; it is the part which, when integrated into self, brings us back into wholeness and our full power.

Shadow work is like time-travelling through the unconscious realms, therefore we can begin to lighten up around it and release some of the fear we hold around the dark, as we understand ourselves to be time- and space-travellers. Each time we expand into the darkness, we are building our capacity to hold life. By embracing the shadow and letting it inform us and move us, it breathes new life into us, it begins to illuminate the depths of what we need to know. If along the way we try to shut it down, we miss the opportunity to grow and evolve. As we honour what has been buried inside, we begin to expand our capacity to hold new levels of awareness within us.

The true nature of the dark shadow is wisdom, if you give it a place to rest its weary feet, so that it may reveal its mysteries to you. The soul will always call us forward to evolve, to claim our shadows, our misplaced desires, our inability to express that which we hold in the dark. But sometimes we let our shadows overshadow us. We become so attached to who we believe ourselves to be, too afraid to step aside and allow a new self to emerge. We become unable to see where we are going or relate to who we have been. This is when we hit a wall and enter into the dark night of the soul, so consumed by the darkness we see no way out.

MY STORY

They say you should never have regrets. But I do. I regret the pain I caused. I regret not knowing there was a softer way to be in life when tending to our trauma. I wish I had known how to be a softer mother in my youth. I wish I'd known that having a child wouldn't give me the love I wanted and needed, that that had to come from myself. I couldn't feel the joy that motherhood promised to me. Numbing my pain kept me in a state of inertia. I don't regret in order to beat myself up, but to be truthful with myself. To acknowledge that our healing moves in cycles and spirals, and those deep-seated wounds take time to be excavated, and sometimes they never will be. I live with the consequences of my trauma daily. I live with the knowledge that for most of my adult and younger life my nervous system was profoundly dysregulated, and this caused me to miss out on so much.

Now I can hold myself tenderly and softly through it all and I can do the same for others. Our softness is needed at this time. We have too much harm in the world as it is and it is not the way of the compassionate mother. Yes, sometimes the Mother is fierce as fuck. Yet in surrender we come back into the natural flow of life. Nature is a fierce force but her rebalancing is never done out of malice, it is to bring us and the Earth back into balance.

I have come to understand that it is no longer about what we want to happen, but what needs to happen for the greater good of all. This isn't to bypass what is in front of us. It's how I feel and see the flow of universal law at play. One of the reasons I am so passionate about being in service to the Mother is because I know the magic of being plugged back into Her.

The Dark Night of the Soul

We each reach a point in our lives when the things that have made us feel fulfilled no longer do. I often think of it like some kind of biological internal clock that goes off as we hit certain milestones in life. Something in us switches on and the soul begins to call us inwards to look at what we have created in our lives. For some of us this turns into a dark night of the soul. We are left feeling lost because all we created doesn't bring us any real joy. We realise that we have been living in a limited way and not tapping into our fullest potential.

When the soul wants alignment, you will know. You will experience a feeling of dissatisfaction or that there is something missing. The soul is an aspect of you that is aligned with you on a level of magic and innovation. It holds the truth of your potential; it knows the truth of who you are to grow into and become. Its role is to steer you away from the humdrum of your limited human experience. Away from the false image of you that may have grown through conditioned beliefs based on what someone else taught you to be.

The soul carries a vision for your life, it sees more than you ever could. It holds the blueprint of your true gifts and natural abilities. All you have to do is figure out along the way how to let this unfolding happen naturally, how to build a bridge between your divine and human self, between the magic and the mundane. Through the soul we have access to universal wisdom. We have access to the field of intelligence of the Mother. The soul could be seen as the motherboard of life that holds all relevant information and codes. Like the control centre of a computer system, the field of the Mother is both the missing and essential ingredient we have neglected on a collective level. It is the element that connects all crucial components as well as the peripheral aspects of our lives. It is the web of life that brings all into connection with one another. It is what makes life flow in balance.

The dark night of the soul often creeps in unexpectedly. Like a thief in the night, it steals the life you thought you were comfortable in and shows you all the ways you have been blind to your own unhappiness. It is a gateway your soul walks through to call back all your lost parts. It is a metamorphic process you may think you are not strong enough to face, yet as your life slowly starts to unravel, know that your soul calls it forth only when you are ready for it: the next phase of your growth and expansion is immanent.

Our dark night of the soul can be catalysed through many life events: the loss of a close relationship, the loss of a business or a job. We may be plummeted into the grief at the loss of another. Or we feel the grief of the realisation that we have disowned our own power. We may experience it as a bout of depression, or an unexpected event, but in reality it is a cry from the soul that wants to come through and be embodied. The internal call usually doesn't follow logic or the status quo and often seems impractical or impossible. An insight may arise that you need to move house or be in a certain part of the world for no apparent reason other than you feel it to be true. The deeper call is a quiet voice that will not leave you alone until you yield to it. Your inner being knows the way to a greater more expanded version of you. Dare you let her lead the way? Are you willing for her to dismantle your life? Are you here to create a new edge of human potential that no longer follows the static rules of life?

The dark night of the soul is a liminal space. A time to connect to the unconscious realms of our existence. Our dreamtime can be a powerful ally for this as our dreams hold deep wisdom and hidden messages to inform our curious enquiry into that which we have hidden in the shadows. A place that is dark, a place that is yin, a place that is naturally feminine in nature.

We are currently in a collective dark night of the soul as we are called to shed that which no longer serves our collective. The radical shifts taking place bring with them a loss of identity and the feeling of being lost as you swirl around in the dark without a sense of being able to navigate, yet your soul is always there. The dark is leading you back to it. It seems so far in the distance, a small spark that you must learn to trust in. You always have the power to access that part of yourself who is safe, light, expansive and sovereign. Call her in, open up and surrender: she is calling you to remember who you are.

This experience of the dark night will completely change you. It will show you where you have been playing small and bring forth the assemblance of aspects of the self you have forgotten. Parts you may have abandoned in order to feel safe, belong or not rock the boat. The parts you hid under other people's expectations. The dark night of the soul is a test of faith, surrender and purification. It is a call back to the divine within. An attempt of the soul to bring you closer to your true nature. When the dark night comes knocking it is an opportunity to dialogue with the deeper mystery of life and dissolve into the great void of the darkness: the primordial home of the Mother.

So much of the dark night of the soul is to do with just that – the soul, the essence of your being. The part of you that travels through space and time, lifetime to lifetime, to evolve and grow and experience life. It is the part of you that knows it is part of the very fabric of life and therefore carries a spark of the Mother with it always. Its task is to lead you back to the source of life. It helps you cultivate trust and courage in self and a higher power. You get to be aware of your own power as you are stripped bare and the real you is revealed.

Your soul will always move in the direction of growth and creation. When you lose jobs, relationships, possessions unexpectedly or your life begins to feel stuck, you can guarantee the call of your soul may have had something to do with it. Your soul moves with feminine flow and you can either make the choice consciously or she will make it for you. She brings no guarantees of how the future will flow. You have to move in blind faith and trust. Few choose to live their lives this way. Are you one of the few prepared to follow the call of your soul?

There is no shortcut on your soul's path. Our souls come to experience certain key lessons. The same lessons come round and around until we catch hold. Our soul will ask that we strip naked in front of one another with radical honesty, transparency and vulnerability. Its only impulse to come fully home to itself. It longs for union between body and soul. It will magnetise to you people, places, things in order to ignite your consciousness into greater awareness of who you are. Its trajectory, to always follow the path that leads to being in service to something greater than you currently perceive yourself to be.

The soul has come to reveal itself. To live in a state of naked radiance. The soul relishes all of life's experiences as it is cracked open to the full landscape of you.

The dark night of the soul is a time to have a dialogue with our hidden emotions, to stop holding on to a time when things were different. We have to be willing to step into the unknown to learn to work with the cycles of life. To listen to the deep mystery and dissolve into the great void of Her. When we strip it back it is the soul that is calling us back into the depths of who we are, to be in relationship with Her.

The dark night of the soul has a lot to do with the surrender into the unknown and listening to the deeper call of your heart within. What within you is calling to be heard? What is calling to be loved back into being? What parts of yourself have you neglected or what dreams have you not allowed to pour through into the now? What desires have you let slip away out of your reach and conscious knowing?

EXERCISE

FEELING INTO YOUR DESIRE

Know that there is no race to get to know the deeper parts of yourself: you get there when you get there. Your soul call and the call of the Mother will never not be. We are in a spiralling resolution of evolution that cannot be stopped. Your deepest desires will never not be there. They are not a flippant want. They are a direct directive from the core blueprint of your soul. Your true desires are already imprinted in your bones: a script written long before you were birthed. It is the call that makes your soul sing. Through trial and error we sense, we feel our way into greater alignment.

Here's a set of questions to get you feeling into what is calling you forth. You may choose to write or talk your responses out. The creative arts can offer a great resource for accessing our hidden depths and knowing, for going deeper than our minds think is possible. Using the medium of drawing or painting we can create meaningful abstract messages. Also, the craft of automatic writing works as a process in which we allow the truth of our voice to permeate from behind the chatter of the mind. In these spaces we can begin to see our real relationship with our souls.

- What makes your heart sing, your soul come alive and aligns you to joy?

- What would you do if there were no financial restraints and no one standing in your way?
- Have you ever had a glimpse of connecting to your purpose? It doesn't need to be grand. It can simply be to be more loving or to shift a long-held belief.
- If you don't know, look back to when you were a child, what was the thing you most loved to daydream about?
- What are the activities you may push aside until you have time, but you wish you could do them all the time?
- What do people reflect back to you that you are good at doing or being?

....

Although at first the dark night of the soul looks and feels like death and loss, its purpose is the reclamation of our soul work. The reclamation of our power. The truth of who we are. Our dark night is attached to purpose. Our devotion to that deeper life-spark that pulses from within the depths of our being.

To go all the way in takes our full vigilance. Often because of our fears of the dark we reach a false sense of power and convince ourselves that we have gone all the way in. We may want to pop out of the process before we have fully reached our true power. We hit spots where we find a pocket of pain and think when we touch that we have hit the deeper thing. This is a coping mechanism that developed because of the fear of getting in touch with so much power. It causes us to stay in the shallows of life. When we wallow in the shallows we are buffeted by the waves of life and think that things are getting worse rather than better. But the further we go inward, we actually realise that we can breathe more deeply.

In this space, the realm of the unconscious makes itself known. We are being called back into the body, back into the dark of the womb of creation. A place that has been pushed back into the recesses of life, diminished and obscured from our daily lives because death and the process of constant rebirth have not been revered in our culture as essential parts of our human learning. As the old patterns die away, reform and integrate we have the capacity to fuel and fulfil that which wants to be birthed and brought through us.

As we stand at this pivotal crossroads in the evolution of humanity, and traverse our collective dark night of the soul, so many of us are being called to move through the dark and shed that which no longer serves. The loss of identity will mean radical change for us individually and collectively. The world has been devoid of soul for so long that it is longing to come back into wholeness. And as we stand in our collective dark night of the soul, we have to know that there is no shame attached to the feelings of wanting to die. We must allow ourselves to speak openly, to be transparent, and be seen in our dark days, so we can shine a light on that which truly wants to be transmuted and emerge. We must make it the norm to hold one other in hitting the bottom of the pit so we can begin once again to find solid ground.

MY STORY

The path that led me to my dark night of the soul was a series of events that brought me to my knees. I knew I was working in a way that was burning me out. I had made friendships where I was over-giving. I knew I wasn't being honoured in my relationship. Yet, I couldn't stop myself living from these unhealthy connections. I wouldn't allow myself to believe that I had made that many mistakes by not listening to the deeper call. I had closed down and rejected my soul's calling. At times like this, life truly then has no choice but to step in. How that presents itself can come in many forms. My knock at the door was dramatic. And when the Mother swept in with Her "Enough is enough!" directive, the only thing for me to do was to surrender.

Only now am I fully following the memo that comes with a dark night after giving up my business, my clients and my spiritual teacher. This is the first time I have let go with so much ease. I know the drill now. I know the sensations when the dark creeps in and calls you to relinquish the outdated version of the self. It's a feeling of malaise or melancholy that sets in, or things just don't seem to flow anymore. The company you normally keep seems to grate on you or there are constant misunderstandings or mixed signals taking place. Things just feel misaligned. I have learnt not to see them as wrong anymore but just signs that a shift of soul alignment is coming.

We have to be willing to withdraw into the quiet so we can hear our soul's call.

I didn't listen for a long time and the accumulation of trauma I carried, plus not listening to the messages of my body, created many occurrences of illness. An imbalance in blood sugars (an inability to take in the sweetness of life); Lyme disease (fear of the unknown); chronic fatigue ME (wanting to not participate in life and a loss of passion); lumps in my breast tissue (my loss of faith and lack of nourishment). The way illnesses manifest in my body is always a sign that I have failed to tend to my emotions. Illness has always been a path to my deeper awakening. This may not be the case for everyone. But for me my body screams until I listen and hear its metaphysical messages and take time to mother myself. No matter what level of medical intervention I accept, my body almost never rectifies itself until I tend to it on an energetic level.

I can see how all my ailments were compounded symptoms of being frozen in fear as a child, literally stopping the activity in my body. I have come to believe that the length of time you spend in the underworld is in direct correlation to how much you were not able to be yourself during childhood. This is the place where most of your root wounding takes place. The place where we first begin to hide the truth of who we are as we get layered with programmes passed down by our caregivers, just as they were passed down by theirs. Our job is to unravel the truth from that which is false and step away from the identity we have been moulded to be. As we move through our earthly motherliness we can truly connect with the fullness and love of the Mother.

Death

Soul work is not a high road.
It's a deep fall into an unforgiving
darkness that won't let you go
until you find the song that sings you home.
McCall Erickson

With all transformation we come face to face with death, it can be no other way. Death is a vital part of life. Nature decomposes its matter every winter to bring new life. So it is with us. To die to your old way of being takes courage. The soul will always call us forward to evolve, to claim our shadows. Her call is subtle and we often misinterpret her wisdom as a signal to exit the body – to die physically – rather than to go deeper into it and allow a psychological part of ourselves to die. In all big upgrades the sensation of dying to the old may feel like suicidal tendencies. We may take the signal for death literally. As I did.

In my life I have danced with death a thousand times. It has become my intimate bed fellow. Death is the guiding force of She who asks you to learn to die well and release all that no longer serves. I was never afraid of death until I separated myself from my ancestral culture. In my younger years, when someone died, we would lay them out to rest in a front room. I would watch the women sing over the body, they would wash and dress them and comb their hair as though they were still inhabiting their body. And we would sit round and drink and tell stories about their life. Now all of that has been handed over to funeral homes and we are disconnected from the normal process of dying and grieving.

I get it, in the modern world carving time to go inwards isn't always possible. Yet at this time in humanity can we afford not to make time to listen inward? As we move through these changing times, we will need more than ever the ability to tune inwards to hear wisdom from beyond the veil as the noise of the world grows louder and our sense of what is real and what is artificial becomes more blurred. We will need more than ever our sensitive nature to come back online so that we can feel truth in our bodies.

When we embrace the notion of dying to the old ways, we can see that it is an opportunity to arrive at the threshold of a new version of self. We have to believe, even when the path ahead is dimly lit and we can only see one step ahead, that the Mother is guiding us all the way.

Death is the start of the journey, not the end. Here in her dark womb, you are learning to lighten the load. Learning to hold your heightened senses and the deep well of wisdom within. Learning what it means to be reborn.

Please do not feel you have to figure this out alone. Seek the necessary help. Let's start reframing our desire to die as a pathway to rebirth something new.

MY STORY

Sometimes life becomes so unbearable, the pain in your heart so heavy, the voices in your head so loud that you feel there is no way forward, backwards or even sideways. You become hemmed in by your own maddening thoughts and failing body, and the choice whether to live or die gets taken out of your hands.

In 2018 I reached a crisis point, which literally took me to the brink of death. Like Paulo Coelho's Veronica, I wanted to die. I didn't want to have to face another day. I was tired of feeling lost. I was done with life. I was going home to meet my maker, to have it out with Her. I wanted to know why my life had been so challenging. Why I had experienced so many traumas as a child. This wasn't the life I somehow knew I had come here to live. I had no idea that the urge to die was in fact a call from my soul to leave behind the outdated version of myself and to step into my greatness. This was a wake-up call of epic proportions for me to rise from the ashes of my life and become a shining light for other women to see their own brilliance reflected back. But I didn't know that then. All I knew was that I couldn't live another moment this way.

The chain of events that activated this one of many of my dark nights of the soul was a series of deaths stacked upon one another. I had lost my partner to cancer. My mother had died. I had to let go of my home. I closed down my business. Two of my best friends turned against me… I thought I was taking time out to tend to my grief as more of my life began to slip away. But I had so much fear regarding all that was seemingly being taken away from me. I felt I had no passion or purpose anymore. I woke one day and just wanted to die.

*

The morning of my near death, as the sun gleamed through the window crack signalling the dawning of another day, I was willing my body to die. I lay there feeling the life drain out of me. I heard the constant buzzing of my phone. But I was out of my body, I couldn't respond.

Locked inside my own mind, I was sinking further into a black hole. Unable to respond with words, my body was shutting down.

Message after message arrived from loved ones who sensed something was wrong:

the people who loved me heard my virtual call and caught me just as I hit the bottom. I believe that day was guided by higher forces: circumstances woven together by the universe to create the perfect storm. A set of surreal divinely orchestrated events that brought five people's lives together into one singular convergence.

As the feeling of life began to drain from me. A sweet feeling of contentment washed over me.

Death kissed me on the lips that day, and the Great Mother brought me back to life.

Like sap rising through roots, I felt the rising of a substance move through me as I lay on the bed. I have never felt peace like it. I had never felt love like it. All I knew is that it was the essence of the Great Mother washing me clean. The embrace of Her love penetrated me in a way that flooded every cell with the knowing that life has always had my back despite all the trauma I had been born into and subsequently lived through.

When my body went off-line, my soul detached and the part of me I class as my awareness rested back into a field of intelligence that is the feminine. It is always around us, we have just become numb to its existence. It was like passing through a thin veil, being fine-tuned onto a different radio wavelength, one that can only be reached when the mind is still and we inhabit the body. I began to understand what it was to be in a fully embodied state. I got to sense in a visceral way what it feels like when our soul and our humanness collide.

Prior to that, the accumulated trauma in my body made it almost impossible to really connect to anything in a subtle way. I would easily become dysregulated and have to numb out. Life, in that moment of meeting death, gave me a reboot. I was taken back into a childlike state and felt what it was like to be suspended in the great void before we inhabit this body. It was a state that encapsulates the pure essence of the Great Mother. What was only a split second in Earth time felt like a lifetime of connection. In those valuable moments I was able to sense why my life had been brought to that point. I had lost faith in the divine and cut myself off from being plugged into life. I was trying to fuel myself and getting nowhere fast.

The conversation I had with the Mother as my body lay there was probably only minutes, yet it felt like I visited every experience in this lifetime and beyond. There was no judgement as Her love kept me in suspended animation. I was told that this was my choice. And with those few words I felt like a weight had been lifted from my shoulders. I felt I was let off the hook of feeling like a disappointment for not having found my way sooner. And that the burden of all the demands and restrictions placed on me as a child to follow inappropriate, unpredictable and unattainable rules began to melt away.

This was the acceptance I had needed all along. To just be able to be myself, even if that meant dying felt like the best option. It was the first time I ever felt I was able to make a choice just for myself. And with that I immediately knew I wanted to live. I knew that in some extreme way this was the beginning of me finding my voice and hearing my truth.

The road back to finding oneself can be a long and dangerous one. I don't recommend the way I did it. Yet I do know that so many during these changing times feel the call of death at the door. I am here to say it doesn't mean literal death when you feel it. It is calling you to let go of an outdated identity and surrender to the deep love of the Mother that is calling us home.

EXERCISE

DEATH RITUAL

You do not have to go to the extremes my soul took me to in order to find out more of your soul path or reconnect to your deeper sense of purpose. You can take yourself through a death ritual where you imagine looking back on your life as if you had died. When we imagine a life lived void of the things we love, when we reflect on what we wished we had done but did not, when we imagine ourselves decaying in the ground returning back to Source, we gain important perspectives. You can reflect on whether you were fully loved. Did you leave a lasting impression on others or fade into obscurity? Did your life have meaning? Do you want more from your life?

We can use our imagination to gain a deeper look into our inner world. The times when we are between waking and sleeping tend to be when we are more attuned to the unseen.

Lie down in a dark place with the conscious intention that you are going to be shown how life would be should you leave it behind.

Allow your awareness to sink back into the body and count down from 100 to 0, syncing your breath in time to the numbers, holding the intention that when 0 is reached you will see clearly the inner workings of your psyche.

If numbers aren't your thing just follow the inward and outward motion of the breath with the intention that with each full breath your inner knowing will be revealed to you.

Let your imagination flow, let yourself be led in the unfolding of what your life would be like if you were no longer living it. Imagine what it may feel like to let your life force wane. To see yourself floating above your own funeral. What is being said about who you are/were as a being? Is there love, delight or regret? If fear arises, speak gently to that part of you that may be confused by your intentions to court the notion of death. Know that you are in control throughout the whole process.

What emotions are you becoming aware of? Do you need to cry or wail, shout or scream? Allow yourself to go there, to let yourself feel and have it all.

When you are done, record your experience. What is desiring to be expressed? Speak from the heart not the head. Let yourself be free with your expression. What was brought to light? What needs to be let go of? What no longer resonates with the woman you are becoming? What are you grateful for? What do you cherish and want to keep?

There may be things you didn't know you wanted or desired in your life. Take your time. Allow the voice of your deeper self to have its say. Don't censor or block your flow.

When this process feels complete, shake out your body and prepare yourself for a good night's sleep.

You may want to set the intention for further insights to be revealed through your dreams that can be recorded as you awaken.

If doing this feels too much, you can always just go inwards whilst fully lucid. Ask yourself: What would I like to experience now in my life? See what answers arise.

....

Dear Woman,

Your body is a gateway into the universal realm of the Great Mother

In ancient times we knew how to tap into Her cosmic and earthy realms of creation.

It is Her raw primal energy that connects you to the very spark of life.

Do you remember what it feels like to have that much energy coursing through your body?

Can you remember how expanded and multidimensional you were before you entered this realm?

You have the potency of all the universal possibilities contained within your body,

Can you feel it?

PART THREE

RADIANT

Dear Woman,

We believed the lies we were told about the magnificence of our bodies.

We swam in the dirty waters of the current reality and expected to come out clean.

There has been a mass disembodiment between heart and sex,

We have been bamboozled into abandoning our innocent erotic flow.

We hide so much of our aliveness, our radiance in order to fit in.

Know as Woman you are the portal. You can welcome in all of life.

The Potency of Woman

Woman, you have the potency of all creation in your body. The universe is always seeking to expand within you and outside of you because you are an expression of it. What woman would you need to be to become a part of that vastness? To be the ocean, not just a drop in the ocean? We have the intelligence of many star systems and organic plant life moving through us. When we are able to access that as a visceral embodied memory, we get to reconnect to the vast unknown.

The wisdom of Woman has never been more needed on the planet. There has been so much distortion when it comes to the understanding of what it means to be a woman. Our ancestors were forbidden from practicing their traditions and had to hide their medicine behind closed doors. Yet the wisdom of our lineage can never be lost. It is deep in our hearts and deep in our cells waiting for an activation so we can open up to let Her all the way in. She who traces back to the Original Woman. She who lives through us. She who is us. Our vessels are the conduit through which Her replenishment is reoccurring.

We cannot logic our way into being with Her. We have to enter through the wisdom of the body. Something we have been taught to distrust as women. Just as we have been taught to fear the dark. We have been taught to override ourselves and push past where we are truly at. We are healing the lineage and our ancestors. It isn't always easy to do so, as our world loves to pull us into more disembodied states. We have created lifestyles that have us override the body: we sit in offices or classrooms all day, we work unreasonable hours, tether ourselves to technology, detach from nature and the elements. We have learned to modify our behaviour to play the good girl, the people pleaser. We learned to mimic the feminine through a fabricated social construct that mistakes the feminine for femininity. They are not the same. Femininity is a parody of Her: a submissive and fawning strategy so we can be liked as we suppress our full range of emotions and the power of our voices and wombs. When I speak of the feminine, I am not talking of the man-made construct of femininity that focuses more on the outside appearance of women, that infantilises women and has a desire to keep them young and maiden-like. Nor about feminised behaviour that leans towards being coy or submissive. What I speak of here is a multilayered, formless energy that is beyond behaviours and attitudes: a force that ignites our internal senses and connects us to all life. We forget that the feminine is a chaotic force. One that sweeps in like a tornado as She rearranges your life and strips away all that no longer serves. It is the force of creation, the power of Mother Nature that resides over the cycles of death and rebirth. She is far too vast for one person to conceive of. We each carry a seed, a fractal of Her imprint and as She moves through each of us, together we create a full picture of the whole.

Our current reality does not value the embodiment of the fullness of womanhood, it does not value the feminine. It uses the body of Woman for its own gain. The body has become a commodity, something to own. The use of the body has become for the benefit of the few and has built a world on destructive principles rather that restorative ones.

We live in a world where the female body is still shrouded in shame. Labiaplasty is on the rise amongst our young women. They have little or no idea of the true beauty of their bodies, that every fold, every crease, every ruffle is designed to be there for a reason. They are the fleshy gateways that hold deep wisdom in their tissues. They are the pages of our living library. Our deeper gnosis.

Do not let the current materialistic narrative exile you from your body. We do not have to walk this land as nomads of our own bodies. To think otherwise is to say that somehow Mother Nature got us wrong.

In embracing our embodiment we begin to recognise our indivisibility from nature. We begin to tune in with our greatest power of sensitivity that allows us to enhance our ability to feel ourselves as a part of life through our senses. We begin to tap into the pulse of Her rising up through the Earth and our bodies. We remember why we are here and this knowing trickles down to our girls, our men and our boys. Embodiment is key for these coming times so that we have full use of our life force. The world needs embodied women.

The realm of the body is part of the unknown mystery of the feminine and how we can access the intelligence of the Mother. Our bodies respond to the way we speak to them, and when invited to unlock their intelligence, they will. We can begin by having a conversation with our body and simply ask: "How connected am I to the living matter of earth and cosmos?" and see what answers arise.

Through the body of woman, we bring together cosmic and earthly wisdom that is being held in the land. Through the portal of our womb and pussy we have the capability to elevate this wisdom. If every womb was switched on and aligned with the portals of pussy, heart and throat, the landscape we see outside of us would be very different. Through our bodies we have the ability to shift reality. Our body is a living technology that enables us to tap into the energetic field around us multidimensionally through space and time.

Simultaneously, we are powering up the Earth grids through the core of our bodies which in turn activates our multidimensional nature. As both our and the Earth's frequencies accelerate in intensity it is so important to get acquainted with how the energies of your body flow.

When we first begin to attune to the frequencies of the Mother it may feel like we are being drawn down into the earth. But we are not going anywhere: we are the bridge between the worlds. Unlike in the past when we may have connected with other realms, we took our presence out of the body to travel there. Now we are learning to be embodied here and now and bring the essence of other realms into this realm of existence as the old structures fall away. We are dreaming the coherent reality into existence. This isn't fantasy: rather it is using our imagination to align with the truth that is calling to be birthed through our bodies. Each of us is bringing forth a unique fractal of the whole, igniting and aligning with the original templates of creation.

....

EXERCISE

EMBODYING THE MOTHER

If you have never had a deep relationship with the Mother, you may be surprised to learn the simplicity of the gateways through which you can reach Her. The Mother loves simplicity. She has encoded in us the portals through which to reach Her.

When you shift your focus inwards and place your attention all the way back and rest in the back of the body, you will begin to reorientate yourself to the field of the feminine. We are so conditioned in this fast-paced world to have all of our energy and attention pushed to the front plane of the body. This simple act of shifting your orientation to reside in the back of the body can create enough space for your deeper wisdom to be heard. Coupled with our breath greater access can occur, for the Mother is the breath of life.

....

Dear Woman,

Do not be afraid to go in, to reconnect to the ancient coding.

Drop deeper into self-love, into the sacredness of your being.

Remind yourself that this is not about embracing a method or technique,

It is about cultivating a relationship with Her, with no agenda.

Woman, take time daily to connect to your womb centre.

Place your hands on your belly and heart and ask:

What do I need to do to be a woman who stands fully in her wisdom?

Boundaries

To utilise and hone our sensitivity as a gift of feminine intelligence we need good boundaries. As sensitive children we most likely had our boundaries crossed frequently, whether consciously or unconsciously. With such open fields of energy, we became porous and merged with those around us without knowing how to separate our energy. We may never have felt a sense of autonomy or were given the opportunity to explore ourselves as sovereign beings.

In order to fully open and surrender to Her power, we need to become aware of our boundaries. Boundaries are an act of kindness to yourself and to those around you. They are an extension of your values and the way you want to show up: a clear energetic understanding of where I end and another begins. Boundaries create space in the body for you to breathe and feel. They set an energetic buffer between you and the world.

Creating boundaries moves us to a different shore, away from co-dependency and trauma. When we have had our boundaries violated in the past, there can be a tendency to either erect barriers or not have any boundaries at all. When we establish clear boundaries, we stand in our power and state strongly that which no longer sits right with us. Others may question your new daring stance, your move away from the status quo as you break the victim-perpetrator relationship that has held you small. To them you are rocking the boat. They may not see it as creating a new-found respect for yourself and for them.

Boundaries enable you to see the full dynamics of your relationships. You can see where you stand in the eyes of another. Sometimes that means the relationship ends and sometimes, when you can be with the opening and space created between you, you can form a new dynamic bond. Just like I did with my mother. It requires a softness, a pause to be with what is, so you can see with clear sight all sides of the situation. You can hold the space open for truth to arise with compassion for your raw authentic self.

You cannot step out in a bigger way without clear boundaries. It can feel like a journey filled with peril, especially if you have been a people pleaser and a keeper of the peace. When we shift from outside orientation to one of listening to the call from inside, we begin to hear the wisdom of the body. We may need guidance in this if it is new to us. Ask yourself: "Who can hold me as I take the steps into this new space of being?" A space that holds the blueprint of who you truly are.

Boundaries do not come without growing pains. With clearer boundaries often comes loss. They are the new foundation to rebuild upon. People, places, possessions fall away that no longer resonate with who you are becoming. Boundaries help you clarify what you stand for. You are weeding out the garden so you can see the flowers and beauty of your own creation.

If we as women learnt to create our boundaries to hold more of our own energy from a young age, to hold it without leaking it out, we would naturally cultivate inner safety. You would have a deep well of internal strength that anchors you rooted in your body, so that no one or nothing can make you leave it. This kind of rootedness stems the flow of violence from within and without. When we are rooted in our bodies our fierceness can rise unhindered. We can emit the resounding "No!" of the fierce feminine force from inside of us when we need to. It is essential that we know how to say no without fear of reprisal. It is essential that we know our own minds. Grounding to the earth also helps bring our sensitivity back into balance and enhances our sense of strength as we reconnect back into feeling deeply rooted in ourselves and the organic network of nature. Simply putting our bare feet on the earth helps us reset. Or it can be done via meditation and visualising yourself rooted to the earth.

MY STORY

As a young woman I had a great fear of being in my body. It felt like it was constantly on fire. The kind of burning that comes from frostbite thawing out. I had no buffer, no extra space in my body. I would create more chaos in order to distract me away from sensation, this is the addictive cycle of trauma at play. Destructive chaos felt normal. Even love at that time felt like a threat and I would push that away with extra vigour. Lashing out was my modus operandi. I was on the defence always, my wild inner children never felt safe…even from me. They had no trust in being. They only knew flight or fight. I had no idea how to be with rising feelings. How to be with the raging river of sexual energy that moved through me. It was a force that I came into life with activated, one that only grew as I grew. It was further activated as a consequence of my abuse. After that it leaked out everywhere and into everything, which drew vultures to my door.

EXERCISE

SENSING THE FIELD AROUND YOU

So many of us are sensitive beings and find it hard at times to be in the world because we feel so much. We may find it hard to distinguish enough between what is our energy and what is someone else's. Like untuned antenna we pick up emotions that are not our own. As we learn to distinguish our own energy from that of another's, we begin to identify when intelligence is coming through that is for our betterment rather getting caught in the net of all that is flying around in the collective field. The more we rest into the body the more we enter the realm of the Mother. We feel down to the bones, into the marrow of life.

Do you allow yourself to tune into the more subtle realms of your environment? As you go about your day, think about yourself beyond your physical body. Feel the air upon your skin as you attune to your environment. As you interact with people, places and things notice if they feel different in your bodily awareness. Feel into the subtle differences.

You are like a radio antenna that sends and receives information from others and the universal field of wisdom. To begin to feel life around you on a deeper level requires you to be in a state of receptivity so that you can hear the wisdom that is talking back to you through your subtle awareness, feelings, thoughts and visions. It is like attuning yourself to hear and distinguish a musical note. You have to acclimate yourself to translate the different frequencies of self and others that you come into contact with.

- Take time to sit in stillness for 5 to 10 minutes to start feel the subtle sensations within your body, becoming more aware of your own energy. Move beyond any gross sensations such as pain that may be present, and tune into the more subtle sensations.

- Rub your hands together vigorously then raise them close to your face without touching your skin. Feel the heat generated, feel the energetic signature of your own field. See if you are able to move your hands further away and still sense the energy flow from them.

- Now take that awareness further afield. Tune into someone you know that lives some distance away. Sit quietly as you recall what you feel like when in their presence. Think about the love you have for them and send that their way. (Often when we tune into our intuition in this way the person will reach out if they are also attuned to their inner world.)

Claiming Our Power

Women learn early on to submit to an outside influence rather than claiming their full power. We have been sold a story that to be a woman we need protecting. We have been conditioned to be nice rather than kind, and in doing so we have lost the element of the Mother that holds a fierce energy. Sometimes love is fierce love. The protective mother that will do anything to keep her children from harm. We have turned our anger at the world against ourselves and rendered ourselves incapable. Or we create the narrative of 'them out there': we want to blame the system; we want to blame the men. We find it hard to hold ourselves as Woman accountable. Yet accountability is the medicine for a peaceful life, if not we lose the potency of what we can do as women to change the collective story.

Our internal mothering and our reconnection back to our erotic innocent nature is imperative as we transition through to remembering our wholeness. Bringing both of these energies together – our innocence and our erotic nature – reunites heart and sex: this is real power. Even more so when we unite heart, with pussy, with womb, with throat and drop into communion with the Great Mother.

Now is the time we have to ask how can we tap in and use, rather than misuse, this rich resource of energy. This is a call from the Mother for us to reunite spirit and sex back into the realm of sacredness. To remember that birthing life is a sacred act. That the body is a place of worship and a portal to Her. It is the wellspring from which all life springs forth. That our sexual exchanges can be art in motion, the holiest prayer and communion where we can converge in the heart of life and create the energy of love for the healing of humanity.

Our culture creates women who abandon themselves in order to stay safe. We have sacrificed real safety for a version which is really control. A control of our natural life force, that when held back can only come out in distorted ways. To feel safe, we have to face the layers of betrayal that may be blocking the flow of our power.

The way of the feminine is not about force. It is not like masculine spirituality that tries to have no thoughts, no feelings, to detach and witness. This is a path where we learn to embrace sensation. In so many of our spiritual practices we have been taught to go up and out of the body. There can be no true transformation without the body. It is time that we fully embody Her. We are not escaping the body here, which is an illusion of safety. We are learning to inhabit the body fully, to be fully here. To be fully present with life. To be in a state of surrender. To give yourself grace.

The dismissing of our longing is one of the most painful things we can do to ourselves. We cut the umbilical cord to Her. Our longing is what brings the soul up front and centre. It is a synergistic flow from the divine. Our longing is what will bring life back to the land. It emanates through our hearts, moving us beyond the superficial into the sacred. Our longing is really calling us into service.

When we detach from our longing, we seek out the quick fix, we become addicted to substances, we become constant seekers, unsure of who we are. We need to move beyond the safety of the known and remember what deep longing is. Our deepest longing points us towards true nourishment. It stops us reaching for outside sources of food and overeating to try and quash the hunger we feel inside.

When we don't claim our longing, it shows up in myriad ways. In our dreams and regrets. In our inability to fully engage in the world. Our longing will pull us down into its watery depths until we realise we can breathe under water. We move from the liminal into connection with the soul of the world and stop fighting our true nature.

Society would have us believe it is wrong to want our deepest desires and to long for that which calls us forth into the very fabric of life. We cannot be nourished by Her if we do not allow ourselves to surrender and open to receive Her and follow Her call.

When we open to life, we become supported. Life meets us as we step onto the next level of purpose. When we open to life, everything can literally change overnight, I am testimony to that. Life shifts us into a space-time reality where doors open, gifts appear and opportunities land on our doorstep as we get into alignment with the truth of who we are after being taken to the edge of our identity and shattered open.

The current reality does not and cannot exist without our cooperation and consent. The feminine has been manipulated and the powers-that-be have attempted to destroy Her throughout our history. We are in a time of transition away from the prostitution of feminine energy, of female sexuality, the commercialisation of her beauty and physical form. A time that has left us disconnected, insensitive and ashamed. It is time to explore our bodies, our sexual natures once more. To let life flow through and expand our capacity to hold it all, to be with everything that is present with us now, and all that has been before. It is so easy to meditate our way out of the body; it is a whole new thing to live in the body and anchor our divinity into the body, beyond the noise of life and the mind. It is how we live as full humans: open and as a channel for life.

As we learn to embody the feminine, we invite life to move through us and crack us wide open, so that we can enter into the deeper unknown. To reclaim what is true. To finally complete our missed rites of passage.

We are reclaiming facets we were taught to disembody and leave behind. Alchemising aspects we were taught to fear or denounce.

Obeah. Holy Whore. Witch. Mystic. Oracle. Tantrika. Seer.

Wisdom Keeper. Freedom Lover. Magic Maker. Catalyser.

Reclaiming the true governance of life.

Remembering the reverence of natural laws.

Resurrecting the medicine down in the bones.

EXERCISE

SENSING INTO THE BODY

It is through the sensuous world of the body, through the eyes, ears, skin, muscles and organs that we see and feel and respond to life. The body is the ground through which all our knowing of the world begins. Our instinctual and sensory responses help us discover the ever-changing energetic field around us. When we move out of the head and into the sensory world of the body, we awaken into a slower, deeper landscape beneath the surface of everyday awareness, a landscape of feeling, memory, impulse and dreams. This is where we can begin to feel the rich sensuous world of the Mother.

- Whilst lying down or sitting in a semi-reclined position, place one hand on your lower abdomen and one either on you heart or, if you feel comfortable to do so, rested softly on your pubic mound.

- Bring the awareness to your breath and bring that down to the area of the body your hands are placed on. With each breath take your awareness deeper inwards. Do this for 5-10 minutes

- Bring your awareness to any rising emotion or sensation. Does a tightness take place or a sense of heaviness arise? Where does it stem from in the body? Can you attribute it to an internal organ? Note what you feel. Do this as a daily practice to become more aware of what is moving in you and the state of your being.

The more we attune to the sensations and emotions in the body, the more we can attune to the subtle realms that are communicating back to us. We can also use this level of awareness in practical ways in our lives, not just for connecting to the world from beyond the veil. Life and all that is in it is talking to us all the time. We are in communication with it, this is how we create the collective field around us. When we are more aware of our surroundings, our ability to connect with the world around us expands and we come into deeper intimacy with life.

Dear Woman,

Let the balm of the Mother move through your unique expression
And may it be the elixir that holds you as you expand your capacity to
Hold more of your energy and life force.
As you allow this ecstatic feminine pulse of life to move through you
Ask yourself how deep in your body can you allow it to go?
And ask yourself what woman would you need to be to be
To act as a reflection of the Mother's cosmic force?
A force that penetrates the world with its erotic flow
A sexual sensual impulse that sets all life aglow.

MY STORY

When we have been trained to hide our power, we may be accustomed to turning against our selves, switching off our power as a protection mechanism that kept us in a perceived state of safety. Yet this is often a false sense of safety. The day my mother died I felt that there was something wrong. But I pushed the feeling away. I didn't trust my power and I didn't trust my intuition.

I still wonder if she would have still been alive today if I hadn't squashed that nudge inside to go to her house in the middle the night. I thought what I was sensing, seeing and feeling was a vision and not a premonition. I had been doing some clearing that night, the scope of my gift was unknown to me then. I felt her spirit strongly. Her presence was in the room to the point I was unable to go to sleep until I sat down and wrote a letter of forgiveness to her for all that she was unable to acknowledge. In that moment I realised it didn't really matter, she was who she was. What mattered was that I was able to put down the pain for myself on some level. If I'd have known that that was the last time I would have had some kind of contact with her on this plane of existence then would I have trusted my intuition more deeply.

Intuition

Our intuition is a gift. It is a state of being in which we surrender into receivership and trust of deep knowing to take in what wants to come through us, the skill of sensing and knowing what is coming, before our physical senses know it. It is our most powerful inner compass. Listening to our intuition helps us decode our path and connect to our destiny. When we are open to receiving, we are able to connect to the field of the unseen world. We are able to tap into Her rhythms to feel into why we are here.

What if we saw intuition as something we embody rather than something we have to think about? A connection back to our primal ancestral instinct. Instincts relate to our survival. They are passed down through our DNA, connected to a time when we relied on our senses in a deeper way that enabled us to stay safe. A time when we were connected more to the land and had to use our own internal navigation to move through the world.

Yet, in a modern world where our thinking is taken away from us, we have lost that skill. We hand over our instincts, insights and intuitions to technology and others, when they are our most powerful inner compass.

There have been so many times I have gone against my intuition for fear of reprisal. For fear of not belonging. For fear hurting others. So many of us do this, even when we know that going against our deeper knowing creates unease in the body as we stray further from the truth of who we are.

When we are grounded in our bodies it becomes easier to hear, sense and feel our intuitive nudges. Intuition is like a loving mother that wants to guide you towards self-fulfilment. When we come into stillness, it's as though the whole intelligence of the universe opens for us to connect to. Are you willing to get still enough to listen? Still enough to receive?

Intuition, like the wind, can be gentle or incredibly powerful. Being in the body creates structure and stability for us to receive the information. We then have the ability to hear the messages of support from our soul voice and take our life in the direction it is steering us. Intuition can often feel like it is guiding us down blind alleyways. We get a nudge to go somewhere and it makes no logical sense as to why. Yet we go because deep down we feel it ringing with a truth that resounds in our bones. Sometimes those nudges may not come to flourish straight away. Like bamboo they don't sprout until years later.

All the while, behind the scenes, the universe is putting things into place, rooting down your desires into this reality until you are able to make tangible sense of them. The dark holds so much wisdom and it is often such a necessary part of the journey. We may need to go into the dark to reclaim our wisdom.

EXERCISE

FEELING YOUR YES AND NO

How do we hear our yes and no? How do we tune in? The simplest way to start is to imagine them.

- Think about being asked to do a job for someone, and the first thing that pops up is a no. But your people pleaser part immediately kicks in and so you say yes.

- To know your deeper truth, you can ask yourself: If they forgot about you and asked another person instead would you be relieved or disappointed? And there you have your answer.

- You get to feel what your emotional response would be, rather than the thoughts that may be running through your mind based on self-sabotage or past survival strategies.

This is the key to beginning to listen to the truth of what you truly desire. When the answer arises, do you dare act upon the wisdom given?

When we begin to get quiet and listen to what is revealed from the inside out, we grow our intuitive gifts. We sense, we feel, we know, we grow, we begin to feel the pulse of life that moves through every cell and connects us to its flow. It is the same energy that informs the birds, bees and trees when it's time to shift gear and migrate or shed leaves. It is not a tangible thing. It is a knowing. We learnt to trust in the unseen and the mystery of life. This is terrifying to the mind, the part of us that needs to know in order to feel safe. Faith is the order of the day here, to trust where we are being led. And often it leads us to become completely different people than what we could ever imagine ourselves to be. When we experience a lack of direction it is a sure sign that we have lost our way to receptivity.

EXERCISE

FOLLOWING YOUR NORTH STAR

We can have an inkling of where we are heading, yet the details are not clear. As long as we know where the end point could be, we have a guiding light in the distance to focus on. When I first came across the activations I experienced through hearing the terms tantra, Mother World and Original Woman, they were like beacons in the darkness of my life that awakened a deep remembrance. They helped me to sense the emergence of a future-ancient reality that was unfolding into this world from the unseen realms. They showed a bigger picture unfolding before us: one where life is lived in a harmonic way.

Honing our sensitivity is a skill and one to be developed for these unpredictable times. It is a skill we will need more than ever to be able to navigate the thinning of the veils and the merging of our realities. The first step is knowing how you sense information and the world around you. Do you sense in pictures – clairvoyance – or in sound – clairaudience – or beyond words – clairsentience? As time goes on you will get to know the way your intuition wishes to speak with you through your senses. Intuition and the unseen world speak in symbology. Symbols don't have firm meaning, they are subjective to you.

- Ask a question in your mind and see what arises in response – is it a word, an image or a sense of knowing? What meaning do you give to it? Not the prescribed meaning but what does it mean to you?

- If you do not receive any clear response, then speak your question aloud. When we give words to something we can see clearer and give it more form.

- Ask another question and begin to build a picture of how your wisdom speaks to you. You will be amazed by what arises just by this simple act.

EXERCISE

TAKING STOCK

- Reflect on all the times you have received intuitive hits throughout your life, all the way from your childhood until now.
- Focus on three or four of these incidents in which you sensed the unseen world around you.
- How did the information present itself, where did you feel it in your body?
- Recall the physical environment you were in.
- What activities were you doing when the information came through? Were you talking with another, dreaming, walking alone in nature, driving, making art…?

Each of these questions will help you begin to gain more clarity about how and when you get your intuitive hits. Like with any relationship when we pay attention to the dynamics, it grows and flourishes. It is the same with our intuition, it likes to know we are paying it attention and it primes the mind to be in receptive mode. It also informs you that your intuition talks to you all the time. Ask these questions often to further develop the connection you have to your intuition.

Being in the body is key to connecting deeper to our intuition and soul messages. Our connection to the unseen world isn't about detachment from the physical but being more embedded and grounded in it. All universal and soul wisdom has to travel through the vessel of the body to be received. Your energetic being is always in communication with your environment. To begin to attune to the more subtle realms you can learn to sense into it more by heightening your awareness of that.

We can listen to the call of the soul as an invitation to improve on our out-dated ways of being. When we don't take heed of the soul's call, we can create vast amounts in the world, but there is often a sense of emptiness that comes with it.

We can observe this in the world as the constant production and accumulation of things to fill a void. The void is pointing us to the things we have been trained to ignore: our soul's voice or intuitive and innate guidance. As in my case, feeling so under resourced as a mother pointed me towards the deeper nourishment of the Mother that would lead me to the fulfilment of my soul.

This deeper longing is for the things that are already in your deeper field of awareness, imprinted in your coding. It wouldn't be in your awareness otherwise. You are simply desiring that which is already ordained to you. You recognise it as a deeper soul resonance. If, like a seed, we have all of who we are already encoded in us, the journey then becomes not about fixing or healing ourselves, but understanding that we have been using the essential being of us in an inappropriate way. Know that you already have the gifts you think you need to seek outside of you. Your connection to the Mother has never been broken, you just stopped being able to feel it.

Knowing this, you can let yourself off the hook from thinking that you should know how your path should unfold. Or that implementing your soul gifts should come easy. It doesn't until it does. If you have had little or no experience of doing it before, then of course it is going to take time to learn how to implement the new skills. Of course you are going to make mistakes. This is why cultivating a compassionate heart is essential to your success. You must learn to be soft and gentle with yourself like any mother would with her child when it is learning to walk. She watches them stumble and fall. She doesn't condemn. She encourages through loving intent and she also knows that the child has nothing to learn or to fix, it has an innate ability already in it to walk. And this is how we need to view the journey ahead.

Initiation

We have lost our rites of passage rituals and are ill-equipped as a society to help our teenagers transition into adulthood without causing major distortions. Puberty is a time when hormones begin to awaken. Both sexes entering puberty go through significant thresholds.

Teenagers that have no outlet to explore the raging river of their inner fires become fiery and disorderly when their hormonal elixirs begin to activate. They then turn into adults that have little understanding of their own power and how energy in our bodies works.

When we are brought up to take in a relationship rather than contribute, we create a dynamic that is off-kilter, yet we don't really understand why. It is counter to our truth. We begin to brace for impact, we begin to be over-protective of our own energies for fear of depletion. We begin to become desensitised; we begin to harden. We become fooled into thinking our sensitivity is something to shy away from and our ability to bond with another lessens.

In our culture, sensuality has been assigned to women more so than men. We teach girls by default to be the gatekeepers of intimate touch, whereas boys are taught to be stoically detached from their sensual nature. Brute force replaces feeling when we strive to get ahead in the world and cut ourselves off from sensation.

Often as boys grow, we withdraw parental touch. We teach them that sensuality and sensitivity somehow make them less manly. When parental touch shifts into something that is more standoffish at this delicate time, boys learn that simple cuddles and holding is not a priority or even available. They begin to harden and feel the only place they can get intimate levels of touch is in a relationship, not even amongst their peers, which is more acceptable for girls. They then project their longing needs for connection onto girls way before it is necessary. This creates a world in which men's sexual desire becomes the responsibility of women to regulate. It creates projected ownership of each other's arousal. When in fact we all need to learn about consensual mutual non-sexual touch.

Our boys, as they grow into men, become deprived of necessary loving touch and then seek to get it in inappropriate ways as they too learn to shut down and harden their hearts. Girls, at puberty, are taught a different way to disconnect from their bodies. We tell them not to stand strong in their feminine power when it comes to their sexual life force. We etch into them that the world is a scary place full of predators. Their safety becomes paramount as they learn that they are somehow weaker and should always be afraid of their full sensuality. *Keep it hidden, keep it locked down*, we warn, for fear of reprisal, from subtle remarks to rape. And thus begins the separation of our wild feminine power.

All our children are left with unmet longing. And both sexes venture into adulthood unable to get their needs met without some kind of self-denial. Girls are taught that every problem starts and ends with the female body. And boys determine their worth through their sheer wanting of the female form.

Our young men are taught that their power comes from their loins, they detach from their hearts and become thinking heads driven by pubescent forces. They become men that then believe it's okay to take, because neither sex has been taught how to be fully with their power. Violence erupts as acts of power. We see it everywhere. Men are called weak if they do not comply, shamed into repression away from their true giving nature. Patriarchy begins to become a notion of destruction rather than of protective benevolence, and we create the world we see today.

Our young women learn to cut off from the wisdom of their pussies and wombs. Shamed for being too sexy, they no longer trust themselves, their throat-heart-womb connection is severed. They no longer feel the freedom of having their voices match their feelings, they are taught to think and not feel, they become overburdened with emotions, not knowing how to move them through the body. And all kinds of bodily malfunctions and imbalances arise.

When it comes to our first sexual experiences, what would the world be like if we saw it as a rite of passage? Something our young were initiated in, rather than thrown into with little or no guidance. We have lost so many of our rites of passage when it comes to our beingness and body. A cycle of distortion begins as we hold down the natural unfolding of our human experience.

The initiations that were once performed by the priestesses of the temples, that taught men how to be with women, have long been forgotten. Most men have become clumsy in their attempt to connect with the opposite sex, they lack the knowing of how to be fully present with Woman. They have learnt a language that pays no reverence to the full essence of Woman. This is something which most men have never been shown. When men come up against women, they flounder in our presence and they take. They need us to stand in our power, to hold firm the energy of pussy to womb, to heart to throat. When we open these portals, we are opening up to the essence of the Mother, into a symbiotic relationship with Her. We remember that we are not less than Her, we *are* Her. Our men need the nourishment that comes from the feminine wellspring of the Mother. When they get to experience Her essence embodied, they get to practice being in receivership, and their desire to take shifts.

This is the way of the Mother.

EXERCISE

SENSING YOUR BEINGNESS

- Take a moment to tap into the flow of your life force within: can you feel the pulsing of it in your body? Feel it within you now just as you are. There is nothing to do or change, no goal to achieve, just simply being with yourself. Listen to the sounds around and within you. Embrace any sensations. Follow your breath just as it happens, rising and falling. Feel the breath filling each cell and allow yourself to surrender to the feeling.

- Next you can continue with some focused breathing that brings your awareness to specific areas of the body. Can you feel the sensations that arise in the parts you have connected to?

- To go further still, continue your breathing and place both hands on the body, one on top of the other, resting on your pubic bone. As you breathe in, begin to trace an invisible line up through the centre of your body using one finger all the way up to the top of the head. And as you breathe out trace the finger back down the centre of the body and place it on top of the right hand. Do this for about 10-20 minutes pausing between each breath to sense the sensations that arise.

- Additionally, you can add an extra layer to the breathing exercise. (But know staying with the first layer of just being present with yourself is fine too.) Imagine as you breathe in and down to the base of the body that the opening of your pussy, your labia, are unfurling like the petals of a flower, ever-so slightly. And then as you breathe out and up, they close back ever-so slightly. As you do so, you are drawing up nutrients from the earth to nourish the body of your being, just as a living plant does from the soil. Imagine it to be like the petals of a rose as you gently contract and relax the muscles. This is not a big movement, but a very subtle pulsing motion. You are not doing Kegel exercises here or any movements to add strength. You are doing this to bring more awareness to this area of your body. Do so with no hurry, no real thought in mind, no pushing or forcing the body. Let yourself open with reverence and a new-found curiosity for the layers of this portal. Relax into the present moment with the breath and the subtle movements. Sense the level of receptivity you have to your connection with Mother Earth and Her nourishing resources. Allow the sensations that may arise to begin to move out of the pelvic area up through the body, like sap rising up the stem of a flower. Allow for the natural movement of the body that may occur to happen. If sound wants to come, let it. This is a slow and sensual practice.

....

MY STORY

In the writing of this section, it came to my attention that sex has been the thread that runs through the whole of my life and is the central hub that brings it all together. Sex has dominated every aspect of my life. My path has always been littered with working with sexual energy, from devastation to elevation. It is the thread that has been a constant throughout my whole life.

For a long time, I ran away from my sexuality because I was made to feel it was dangerous. My initiation into sexuality started young in the form of abuse. And my sexual power was overtly activated way before I knew what to do with it.

In my teenage years so much shame was placed upon me for the way my body moved. For the way my body grew. I couldn't correlate at the time because there was so much humiliation directed towards my changing form. I just knew I and it were considered dangerous. The confusion mounted. My body did not feel like my own, not only because of prying hands but because of the messages received from my mother about always covering up. The raging hormonal changes of puberty stoked an anger in me I had never felt before. I lost so much of my voice and sense of self. I think it was around then that I first prayed to God for an answer and help.

The answer came in the form of a book I found hidden in my parents' room. I always knew there was more than what appeared on the surface of life and this book sparked a deep knowing in me about the healing nature of the female body. The book, *Surrogate Wife: The Story of a Masters & Johnson Sexual Therapist and the Nine Cases She Treated* by Valerie X Scott, activated me into a deep knowing that women had initiated men into their sexual opening and that women surrendering their sexual energy and power over to men was the wrong way round. It was the first time that I experienced a flashback to an ancient time when priestesses initiated men in the temples.

It wasn't something I could speak about; it wasn't something I fully cognitively understood. It wasn't something I really wanted to know about in light of what was happening to my body at the time. Yet, that knowing never left me, it rattled around in my psyche for years. It was an echo of a past life, of someone who worked with this life force energy in some other lifetime.

Sexual Energy

There is not one living soul that was not created from sexual energy. We are created through sexual expression, yet we have let ourselves create a narrative that makes us ashamed of our flesh. Our natural sensuality has been made a sin. How many stories about your body have you taken on and made real about your feminine essence, whatever your gender? For so long, women have held down their sexual potency because the world around us either says it needs protecting or that it is dangerous. We have all been traumatised to some extent when it comes to our sexual potency, it is part of the very nature of being birthed into this world where sexual wounding has become the norm.

Our truest nature is sensual and erotically innocent. Think of a baby whose sensual ability to feel the world is magnetised tenfold as it takes in its new surroundings. Initially our sensuality is not sexuality, although that does play a part. As a child when you are born with a potency of power that comes from the sacral, and the only narrative on sex in our culture is so warped, then you begin to believe that something is wrong with you. When you have no guidance or rites to initiate you into the deep understanding that you come from a lineage that could be described as a sexual sacred priestess, you can get lost in the cultural noise on sex.

We often forget that the Mother is sexual too – that the act of creation is a sexual act. When we learned of Creation at the hands of the father god, it took sex out of the equation: Creation becomes desexualised. Sex becomes shamed as bad. Remembering the Mother brings sex – embodied creative energy – back into the very centre of life as a sacred and holy act. After all, the Mother essence created the world and it is through Her creative sexual energy that we will be rebirthed. It is time to relinquish the shame, the embarrassment and embrace our sexual empowerment. When we enter into healing our sexual splits, we come home to the seat of our power – our wombs – and awaken the power there that has been shut down.

In a world where the masculine principle has been conditioned to sacrifice its sensuality in favour of dominance, our sexual nature has become harmful on a mass scale. When we deny our sexual nature and suppress it, it comes out sideways. The very frequency that created us is shied away from, and therefore so is our true nature.

Our stories about sex have been governed by unconscious programs of our parents, ancestors, peers and society, riddled with lust, manipulation, abuse, performance, competition and separation. In a world that wants harder and faster in everything, sex has been pushed upon us in a dysregulating way. We need to get to a place where we can talk more openly about sex, in a way that gives us a broader and wider perspective than the one we currently have. It is one of the most intimate parts of our human lives, yet many have sexual contact with self or another in a way that is devoid of intimacy. The Great Mother is here to show us a new way of connection to intimacy and our sexual power, one that is more in alignment with our true expanded nature as humans. She offers us a reconnection to our erotic innocence. This is the ability to make love to life first and foremost, before we learn to connect with another. She reminds us of the gift of tuning in to the living organic matrix that created all life. A connection that comes from the heart, that leaves us feeling full rather than empty and unfulfilled. When we connect to the pulse of life, we know we are not alone.

*

The body is a collection of electrical and energetic impulses, yet so much of our understanding of our sexual experiences has been confined to the genital area, and we think that this is the way it is supposed to be. When we discourage sexual exploration beyond the physical, we block these natural occurrences of energy flow. Sex that is connective can be healing. It brings balance to the body and reminds it of its optimum health. The energy of sex can be used to regulate and calm the nervous system.

But in our culture we confine our sensual life force to only sexual encounters. We are not taught to move it further than within the genital area of our body, thus cutting us off from its wider capacity to help us deepen into life. We need to stop getting caught up in the notion that sexual energy is always about having a sexual encounter with another. It can also be energy used to create a project, a friendship, a one-off innocent encounter that comes from the heart or our ability to flow with life.

Synergist Energy Exchange (S.E.X.), a term coined by Neale Donald Walsch, in his *Conversations with God* books, happens all the time. The wave of electrical impulses that can occur when the body goes into a full body orgasm, is the same impulse we are meant to feel in our bodies throughout our days. It is the energy that travels along the entire network of the nervous system and is a healing elixir for the whole being. The Traditional Chinese Medicine philosophy behind the meridian system is the closest I have come to being able to describe it: a network of energy lines that bring vitality when unblocked. Yet we have been taught to contract and squeeze instead of open and receive in all areas of life. Waves of energy are meant to move and feed our cells on a daily basis.

This wave of energy I speak to, that can move up the spinal column and out across the network of nerves in the body, is often referred to as *kundalini*. The concept of kundalini energy extends across Vedic, Tantric and Hindu systems. When this vital life force is activated, it moves through the body like a flow of lava, burning away all in its path that isn't truth. It is often seen as a feminine energy because of the way it moves through the body. Yet it holds both masculine and feminine qualities. It translates to 'coiled snake' because when it is dormant it lies coiled at the base of the spine, housed in the sacrum or 'sacred bone'. In the Hindu tradition this energy is often referred to as Shakti, the goddess that represents the feminine principle. The masculine quality of this energy is to hold focus and is referred to as Shiva. The central column is sometimes called the hollow flute and when energy flows through, it also extends beyond the body through the pathways of energy channels in the body. Some say it is activated when we are a full state of presence, centred within ourselves and aligned with the energy all around us.

Connecting to our sexual energy is a way to facilitate the opening and connection to The Mother because She is life force itself in motion. By bringing our focus into the body and turning into the stillness within, we can surrender back into the field of Her intelligence.

MY STORY

For a long time I did not find it easy to accept that a significant part of my role in this life would be working with sexual energy. When you have lived through so many adverse sexual experiences it can be hard initially to see this as part of your mission.

My first ever experience of my sexual energy being something other than what was used in during sexual intercourse was a spontaneous kundalini awakening. Looking back now, I can see that my body had been priming itself for a while to activate. The little pulses I initially felt during my first yoga class experience like Braxton Hicks contractions, a precursor to the real thing. The riding of the snake-like energy that lives coiled in the sacral area and sacrum (our sacred bone) in the body happened quite unexpectedly, opening my senses, switching all my clairsentient abilities on at once. It's hard to say what activated it. Perhaps it was a moment of bliss, just being totally encapsulated in the present moment. I remember being sat in my garden on a bright sunny day – the kids playing, a drink in hand. I remember a rare moment of happiness, being totally content and at peace within myself. Then suddenly I heard a loud drumming noise, which turned out to be a drop of water hitting the floor. It was as though all my senses exploded outwards and I saw sparkling flashes above my head raining down like a shower of stars.

Suddenly I could see, sense and hear all the layers of what others were saying and doing. I could see spirit and other creatures of the unseen world. Suffice to say, this was the most terrifying thing that had ever happened to me. I was an ordinary young mother who was, at the time, addicted to alcohol and amphetamines. From that point on, my life was never the same again. I had cracked through the veil of this reality and the force of life was calling me into Her realm.

Life was extreme challenging for me from that point on – I didn't understand what was happening and neither did those around me. I felt like I was going insane. It was the first time my family took me to mental health services. I was placed under the care of psychiatry and given medication. Nothing short of a rollercoaster ensued from that point.

What was so hard was that I knew that I couldn't speak of the things I was seeing or thinking for fear of being fully committed and not just sent to outpatient care. I was pretty much alone with my thoughts and the growing sensations in my body for many years. And so I learnt to live in two worlds, discounting any strange anomalies. In a similar way that as a child I had learnt to split myself in two to survive my abuse. It didn't feel very different because as a child my sense of my energetic body would often rise out of my physical body and watch as the acts against me took place. So you see, I was used to living between worlds – I just didn't know at the time that this would manifest into something far greater: the ability to see between realms and into the multiverse.

My kundalini experience had me float out of my body and be held by an unseen force of energy. The magic of these experiences is that, although they were intimate in essence, there was no actual physical touch. What I can say is that there was the presence of deep love that took me out of this awareness and into another field of energy. It taught me that there are multiple different frequencies at play simultaneously and we just have to begin to drop into sensing them. I have experienced this field during death too. The weightlessness of being outside the physical realm of reality, out in the widening field of life. I have hit upon it during intense days of meditation and I have been in a similar suspended state in the early days of my abuse. What all these have in common are that they were activated through a charge of sensual life force energy. They activated in me a deeper connection to myself through my body and the experience of being able to lean back into another channel of life that fully supports and holds and nourishes us, a vast field of energy that feeds every cell of our being and is regenerative and renewing.

Life force energy or kundalini moves through the body and when it hits the heart is the essence of pure love. It is so hard to describe, but this love is always there, we are just attuned out of it. In her book *Sexual Awakening for Women*, Shakti Malan describes this as a phenomenon called 'skydancing', in which the energy of love is so vast in your being that it explodes out of you and your body moves involuntarily. You transcend the past and the future and connect to the depth of your soul in the now.

I see my opening as an adult as an opportunity to return to my erotic innocence and to sense the aliveness of the world around me. For so long I saw this as a burden and bought into the narrative that my ability to see beyond the norm was a problem. But I have come to believe that our body's ability to dance with the harm caused to it and the discomfort of that is not always a problem, out of it can be birthed true magic.

EXERCISE

GET OUT OF YOUR HEAD AND INTO YOUR BODY

Unrehearsed movement and dance are a great way to bring our awareness into the body and unlock previously unfelt emotions. Dance helps to bring you into the here and now and into the flow of your feminine essence, it opens the channels to your instinctual and intuitive flow.

Pick one or two songs that you like to move to. As you move:

- Bring your centre of gravity down in to your pelvis.
- Be aware of your breath – it supports the opening of your energetic channels. Different states of breath bring different states of being. Do you need calming long slow breaths to relax or fast shorter breaths to stimulate?
- Sound – using sound connects the lower and upper body and helps to activate areas of the body. Your throat and mouth are intrinsically connected to your hips, womb and pussy.
- Movement – allow the wisdom of the body to arise and move you. Don't think about it. Let the movement arise from your internal space.
- Touch – if you feel the desire to touch parts of the body do so. What quality of touch do you need – tender touch or a firmer hand? Get acquainted with your curves and the physical landscape of your body and the sensations that arise through your touch.
- Remember stillness, it brings presence and deeper awareness of yourself and your internal sensations.
- There is no right or wrong way to do this movement practice. Make it your own, do what feels true for you. Follow the rhythm of your own being. If emotions arise, let them release through the power of your movements.

Dear Woman,

You can open the flood-gates to your inner being.

Your pussy lips are the gateways that tap into frequency of heaven here on earth.

And as you go deeper into your inner sanctum

The cervix becomes the doorway that takes you into the temple of the womb,

A place where you become privy to all universal truths.

If all women connected to this part of their bodies

Can you imagine the surge of energy that would be present here now?

Tantra

Shakti energy is the divine feminine expression of power. It is the awakening force that brings us into relationship with creation. Shakti is the interweaving of the divine in the physical world and is animated in the outside world through our bodies. It is available to us in every given moment.

When it moves through us, we see that we are not separate from life but part of it. And we see we do not have to push our way through life, direct or control it, which we have learnt to do, based on our patriarchal conditioning that disconnects us from our divine source – the Mother of all life.

We often numb our feelings, sensations and desires and our power which inhibits the shakti flowing through us and out into the world. It is essential for women to begin to reconnect with this energy that rises up through the earth, up through our bodies via the portals of pussy, womb, heart and throat. We become her vessels. It's time to open ourselves radically and unapologetically to our divine shakti force.

In traditional Hindu tantra, shakti is represented by a goddess who stands for this feminine principle of creative power and is often thought of as our sexual power. Yet, as I have experienced it, it is way beyond how we generally perceive sexual power, portrayed out in the world as something that is used for connection in intimate relationships, rather than the vast creative force of energy it truly is.

Tantra is a path of awakening that sees our sexual energy as a potent force for our awakening. It helps us dive into the subconscious of our being and takes us into the realm of the feeling. It helps us bring the hidden aspects of self to light.

MY STORY

Throughout my life it was the (spontaneous) awakening and activation of my shakti energy that was the gateway through which the Mother came in order to lead me back to the truth of who I am. Across the course of my life seeds were planted long before I knew what this energy was. This life force energy that has always been overly active in me. There was nothing I really needed to do for it to be alive. It was and is a deep integral part of who I am and how my body is constructed. From being a young girl, I carried a potent sensual presence. Because this world doesn't know how to hold reverence for that, my childhood was a very confusing time.

I knew far more about it than I should have at that age. I was both fearful and fascinated by its power. It felt familiar to me, yet I had no language for it and any questions were immediately shut down with disgust at my inquisitive mind. It also brought me unwanted attention and harm. At some point, I decided (unconsciously) to shut it down and inadvertently closed down my calling.

*

When the word tantra first came to me, I had no idea what it meant. It dropped into my consciousness fully formed, several months before my kundalini awakening. I ignored it, until one day I was stood in a discount bookstore and there in front of me was a book called *Tantra – the art of mind-blowing sex* by Val Sampson. It had a dull brown cover, but to me it looked illuminated. I grabbed it and took it home. As I read the first few pages it didn't really resonate with the feeling I had initially got from looking at it, so I put it down.

On some level I knew it wasn't on the same vibe as the tantra my spirit was trying to awaken a remembrance of. It had a flavour of what is called 'neo-tantra', a modernised version which is often more about titillation than finding the deeper meaning of self and life. The book's main focus was based on improving sex for bliss, whereas the tantra I knew deep in my soul was not about being in a blissful state but in fact about the unravelling and revealing of the shadow to reveal the depths of who we are.

The feeling that there was more for me to explore never left me, so I picked the book back up. It both intrigued and confronted me. The book talked about exploring one's sexuality with strangers, which was an absolute no-no for me. Not because I am not open to exploring sexual encounters, but because I knew I was here for a different kind of relating. I put tantra out of my mind for some time until the death of my mother. The catalyst that finally got me back on my path was a long dark night of the soul and illness which sent me on a healing path. I ended up on a ten-day silent meditation retreat and met someone there who mentioned tantra. But yet again, the way he spoke about tantra did not appeal to me: I wanted nothing to do with it. This kept happening. For months, random conversations with people would somehow have that word in it. I kind of got the message that this wasn't going to leave me alone.

Then I began to get sick. I know now that it was from not listening to my calling, as well as the shock of how my mother died. I felt lost. I had been in bed for days if not weeks when I had an apparition of Jesus on the edge of my bed. I will never forget it because it wasn't just visual, it was physical too. As I lay in bed, my back turned to the door and head covered with a blanket, I felt someone or something come into the room. I felt the weight of them sit on the bed. And then there was silence. I waited and waited. I thought it was my partner and wondered why he wasn't saying anything. The frustration in me was mounting, so I turned to see why he wasn't speaking.

What I saw was a transparent figure at the end of my bed. He reminded me of the Jesus from the 1999 movie *Dogma*: black, funny and full of sass. Nothing like I would have envisioned him to be. I immediately paid attention, I sat up and tuned in. He spoke to me telepathically of healing sexual wounds. He spoke to me of his union with Mary Magdalene. He spoke to me of having ego and that it is okay to have a strong sense of self. He told me that my role was to help heal the sexual wounds of the planet (I had no idea what he meant). And he too mentioned the word 'tantra'. The way he spoke about it, I knew it was reminiscent of what I felt as a young girl and having our life force energy connect to the source of all life. It was validating.

He told me to get out of bed or else I would die. He came to me over a series of days after that and sat by me as I slowly brought myself back to life. He helped me gain the strength in my legs. And during that time, he helped me find a belief in myself I never knew I had.

The way he spoke made so much sense to me. He told me about the energy of shakti, the primal life force that runs through life, and that it was something I must seek. And don't you know it, I didn't seek – it found me! A pamphlet came through my door a few days later and it had an advert in its back pages for a healing centre in the next village. As I went to look up a meditation class, there on the website was a class called Shakti Dance. I knew I had to be there that night.

When I arrived, I felt so out of my comfort zone amongst the circle of women there. I knew no one. It was so foreign to me as we sat around on the floor and the circle was opened with some kind of prayer. When the facilitator started talking about the dance, that it was done with closed eyes and no steps, I began to relax a little. That was until the music started and many of the women started to disrobe! A part of me started to panic and wanted to bolt from the room. But another part of me knew I was home.

Dancing to music in a way where there was no expectation to perform was exhilarating. We were instructed to just follow the flow of our bodies. I cried the whole way through the class as the other women wailed and howled and screamed and expressed themselves in ways I had never allowed myself to until now. At the end of the dance, we sat back in circle and shared about our experience again. I had never seen women express themselves so openly and vulnerably about things going on in their lives and about their bodies and what moved for them through the dance. It was such an out-of-body mystical experience for me. Suffice to say during that class I spoke for the first time about the pain in my heart around my mother's death and the visitation I had had from Jesus and what he said. I thought I may be looked at weirdly. But no, I was fully received.

The woman leading the class in matter-of-fact way said to me, "You need to meet my teacher, Shakti Malan. She is visiting the UK in a couple of weeks … which she rarely does as she is based in South Africa." It was one of those surreal dream-like moments that makes you realise there is something far greater guiding this whole process. We are fully looked after when we finally choose to listen and follow the internal nudges and participate with life. As you can see, I am a stubborn kind of gal and life always has to send me some quite intense experiences to get me to listen to my greater truth!

And thus, my journey with my flavour of tantra began out in the world. A couple of weeks later I drove to Scotland to participate in a retreat called "Sexual Awakening for Women", with my first-ever teacher Shakti Malan. The year was 2012. And it was an introduction to tantra that wasn't about better sex or being with another. It was about exploring my own sexual energy for self-healing and deeper self-realisation.

During her retreat was the first time I heard the word 'transmission'. I had no idea what the other women meant when I asked them why they were here and they said it was to receive the transmission of energy from Shakti Malan. Tantra teachings are passed down through transmission, through the energetics of the body and connection on a soul level. It is an immediate download of information where you get to sense and feel the truth unlock in your own being as it is passed on by osmosis through the teacher's body and being. At the time when tantra re-entered my life, it was a new concept to me on a mental level but on a physical level I knew I was returning home.

Several years later I came across the work of The Authentic School of Tantra and its founder Devi Ward Erickson's findings on tantra called "The Roots of African Tantra". Everything began to drop into my being in a deeper way after that. I began to have cellular memories rise up in the form of both pictures and sensations which dropped me into a deeper homecoming. I had a new North Star to guide me further on my path.

Devi discovered that the roots of tantra can be traced as far back as 8-10,000 BC to an area of Northern India referred to as the Indus Valley. This valley was the home to a flourishing civilisation founded by Africans that had migrated from Ethiopia, Nubia and Sudan as indicated by archaeological, genetic and linguistic evidence. The people of which were called the Dravidians and they brought tantra with them to that region. They created and cultivated a harmonious matriarchal society.

The tantra that we know today, which is woven with the Vedic tradition of India, only happened in our more recent past, approximately 5000 years ago, when this region was invaded by the Aryans who desecrated the Dravidian culture. Before this happened, the root of the Dravidian people's tantric philosophy was animism and its underlying principle was that:

"All of life is sacred. Everything that we see in this external world is an emanation of the Divine. Every plant, rock, animal, human being is sacred and we are made of the same substance… we are all one."[*]

The fundamental foundation of the Dravidian belief system, from which tantra originally grew, was based on the worship of the Great Mother, the Goddess; it was about worshipping women and the female form. This root of tantra is not commonly or widely spoken about, even though the genetic and archaeological evidence shows that the origins of tantra stemmed from African people.

As a black woman making the link between Africa and tantra only deepened my devotion to the path and the Mother. I see Africa as a rich and fertile land that holds the abundance of the Mother's codes. It is teaming with creative erotic energy,

---

[*]   Devi Ward, "The Roots of African Tantra"

abundant with resources which have been overused and taken for centuries. Just like the feminine, it has been ravaged of its material resources.

*

For me, like so many, tantra has been a way to come back home to the body, to stabilise and metabolise energy and feelings. It has helped me walk through the fire and open to the deeper mysteries of life. For so long women have been given the responsibility of guarding their sexuality against the advances of outside forces. Our bodies have been seen as objects and shrouded in guilt and shame.

The tantric knowing that came to me had more of a feminine flow. It was more of an awareness of being born tantric rather than something I had to learn. Much like having a healing gift, it is an innate gift, already built in. The knowing of tantric origins coming from Africa was a healing of my bloodline and lineage and only deepened when She, the Great Mother, arrived in my life.

Tantra opened my eyes to see the body as a vehicle for my awakening. It showed me life is an ebb and flow, much like the infinity symbol. I respond to life and life responds to me: it is a symbiotic relationship: creation in motion.

*

The feminine heart has been bleeding because of our disconnection from the land. Just before Covid hit I had a huge awakening in which I was guided by an internal voice to go lie on the land and receive information. The information I got was of a tantric nature and a deepening of my understanding that it was more ancient than originally thought. I have always known that tantra was never about a set of techniques, rather it is a way of being that allows for true connection. I was born with this deeper knowing. It sits in my bones. A way of being intimate with self, life and others. It is a container that allows for the whole of our being to be seen, felt and heard. Ultimately tantra is love: a way of finding depth and fulfilment in all aspects of life. It is love that comes direct from the Mother, who teaches us not to be afraid of what is real and what needs to die.

Intimate Connection

Sex is so much more and so much deeper than just learning to sustain orgasms and pleasure and personal relationships. It is connected to the land and the trees, to the rivers and oceans. Our sexuality is the lens through which we perceive all our issues: power and control, pleasure and passions, our desires and wants, our identity or our concept of self.

The body is a doorway. And for survivors of early trauma and abuse that doorway is open wide way before its time, causing the body to be overly sensitive, both cognitively and physically. When we learn to see deep into our experiences on an energetic level, we begin to see that these traits can be harnessed into super powers. This was something I understood intimately as a child. I seemed to notice more, I was more aware of the nuances of taste, smell, sound and texture around me. I could feel the whispers of the wind on my skin and know it was speaking to me. I became highly attuned to my surroundings. I could feel the subtle fluctuations of energy around me. I had been cracked open and in an obscure way connected to the more subtle realms of life.

We have been taught that the body and mind are separate, and that sex and spirit are split. When we look closer, we see how inaccurate that is. It is through our connection to the depths of the body that our primal erotic energy – the energy that brings forth life – resides. And this energy animates all systems in the body. It is the same energy that animates our natural world. In rudimentary terms, when nature is referred to as the 'birds and the bees' it is this erotic pulse they speak of. But, like most areas of life, we split it off and shut it down. In women it becomes the virgin/whore split: a heart and sex disconnect. In the world it becomes greed: we take without reverence for our natural resources. It is impossible for us to stand in our full radiance without it.

Radical change is needed when it comes to how we view intimacy, love and connection. Sex has the ability to regenerate the human body – it is after all the energy that created life – in fact this is its main function. Sex is way beyond the physical. Sex, in loving connection, can be profound and elevate us in a transcendental way, connecting us to cosmic energies all around us.

*

When we are not attuned to being in our bodies, we will always find it hard to know how to fully navigate through life from a place of devotion to it. When we attune to our being we can attune to life. We begin to move into acceptance of how much we have to slow down. The feminine moves slowly but we are trained to override that. This isn't about blaming the patriarchal system we live in, it is about recognising that the world we have built is overtly orientated toward bigger and faster meaning better. We as a collective have to be the ones to stop treating ourselves in this way. We have to stop believing in the narrative that extraction is sexy. That the accumulation of more somehow makes us more. These limiting beliefs keep us striving to get and attain more, only to then realise it is an empty pursuit. We become empty vessels filled with distortion and shadows.

'Father' of Western psychology, Sigmund Freud, observed that we split woman into the categories of either Madonna or whore – virgin mother or promiscuous vixen. His discourse centred on the opinion that women couldn't be both in the eyes of their partners. And as a collective we devoured these messages as truths that have stunted us from becoming fully realised sexually beings, full of vitality and fertility.

Being a fully embodied Woman is being a living technology that the world has been missing for far too long. So much about our bodies and sexuality has been a mystery, so much information and wisdom has been buried or lost along the way. When we think that the full structure of the clitoris was only discovered in 1998, we have to ask "Why? Why did it take so long to formally recognise the existence of a key part of women's sexual anatomy? And why is its full function still not known?" It is an organ in the body that helps to stabilise the functioning of the pelvic floor. It keeps the tissues of the vagina healthy and lubricated. As well as being the only organ in the body dedicated to pleasure. We are not taught this as the norm, because it is not even a consideration in the field of conventional medicine. In fact, it is rarely spoken about except in a sexual way. Thankfully, this is changing: there are many amazing women out there doing work that centres around familiarising ourselves with our female bodies[*].

When we don't take up space in our bodies, other people's values will. What

---

[*] Vaginal mapping is a technique that helps women to get intimate with the external and internal anatomy of their pussies. Carly Rea Beaudry is one such woman I would recommend. I also offer work that centres on getting more deeply intimate with your pussy and womb as an embodiment practice.

can be more precious than taking ownership of our sovereign sensual and sexual self? We get told to be careful and keep ourselves safe because this energy we carry as women is a hot commodity that is irresistible to the male population and their only desire is to devour it. The good girl message rings loudly when it comes to our potency. *Be respectable, keep your legs closed, don't have too many partners, present yourself well for the male gaze because the world is a scary place as a woman alone.* Do you know the dissonance that creates in the body? It shuts off so much of our flow. It creates empty space in the body and when there is empty space it leaves room for outside influences to come in. Closed-down women create a hungry depleted environment.

Because of how both sexes were raised, so much of the way we interact with sexual energy currently has become parasitic with people feeding off one another, and feeding off life, rather than enriching one another. It has accumulated in the silencing of voices and the objectification of the sexes. Where men have to uphold restrictive conditioning that stops them from fully surrendering to life in case they feel they diminish their manhood. And women feel they are always in protection mode, endlessly defending themselves. Men usually go outwards with their distortions; women usually turn them in on themselves and thus the split between the masculine and feminine starts from within. Men get trapped in their addictive desires and women in their deeper longing. When we learn to deny our desires, we learn to manipulate instead. The challenge moving forward to birthing something new is to embrace all of it with loving intent. To give gratitude and give it forgiveness and let our collective pain become the rocket fuel to catalyse change. Let us put down our arms, we don't want these inherent patterns going down our blood lines anymore.

For many who lean more into the frequency of the masculine, their conditioning takes them down a path away from the full range of their emotionality. They will look to the feminine to fill the gaps, trying to fill a void that cannot be fulfilled through another. All of us are born to love, be loved and to be love. That is what we are here for: to find the parts of ourselves that lead us back to love. And so often it is the cracking of our beings that comes from trauma which begins the whole process of alchemy.

So many of the men I worked with as a Tantrika had a desire to rest upon breasts. They came to feel held, to receive nourishment. When a man stands in front of a woman in her full shakti, he cannot but fall to his knees. A part of him dies in the darkness of her connection to the void of the feminine. He is pulled into the Cosmic Womb: an internal pull from his own soul's longing that brings him face-to-face with the death of his ego. He needs the strength of the feminine in her full centred being to hold him when he does. He is rebirthed through the portal of Her back into light with his feminine intact.

Most men do not harm intentionally. They do so because they are depleted of their own feminine essence. We have to stop projecting onto them that all men are either saviours or perpetrators. What is needed is our open hearts, our undivided love and attention, our switched-on wombs and our ignited pussies to lead them back home to the Mother.

*

Sex without the Mother frequency, without love and nurturance, can turn into an empty pursuit. Just like the way we hold a lack of reverence for the Earth, we can mirror that when it comes to connecting to our sex. And for both it comes down to our inability to let ourselves feel deeply. One of the biggest reasons why intimacy becomes fearful for some is because it triggers our emotional blocks and activates our inner children. They so often come out in sexual connections because we touch upon our core energy. Our wounding often touches the heart and when it first opens through intimate sensations, we are taken into our emotional landscape and the things we have hidden away in the body. They come from the inner child who has needs that were not tended to.

To ask for those needs to be met in relationship with another can be uncomfortable, especially if we have not had our needs met in the past. Needs are non-negotiables: we must be clear on what they are. Yet we may never have given what we need to ourselves or even dared ask for it from another, because of our fear of abandonment. In the process of healing, we have to become our own mother-figure and say to the ones inside that it is okay to have our needs met. In doing so we let down the defences that have guarded our erotic flow.

Our cultural fear of intimacy has affected our ability to receive. We tend to fear closeness with strangers, we fear our vulnerability and emotionality. As women we have been told we are "too much" if we go to the depths of our emotions and men have been told they are "too soft" if they do. Compounded isolation and separation are created from this standpoint.

The whole of our being is meant to be in communion and communication with each other and all life. Yet we have closed down so much of our ability to be intimate.

It is okay to open to all of you. To let the light on your skin and to share the parts of you that have been hidden in the dark. We are the alchemists and we have the power to turn lead into gold. We have the capacity to shift the focus of what we create. We are master creators. And as we journey through these changing times, there is redemption, there is resurrection and it comes when we embrace forgiving ourselves and holding ourselves with radical compassion. When we truly embrace the fullness of all that we are, the light and the dark.

EXERCISE

YOUR INNER TEMPLE

When we see our inner space as sacred, we will want to treat it as a temple. We deeply honour it and those who enter there. And in name of that honour, we can imagine ourselves doing a clearing, just as we would clear and clean up any space we occupied as our home. We get to imagine our womb and its entry portal, our pussy, as beautiful temple spaces filled with love and the power of our truest essence.

Both have a magnetic pull and are creative vortexes. They hold nourishment, enriching smells, tastes, rest, rejuvenation and restoration to all those that enter, including yourself. When we view them this way, we can see that a regular energetic cleansing practice is a valuable tool to keep yourself aligned and centred.

Our relationship with our sexual centres can become cluttered with our sexual, personal and relational history, as well as old beliefs and experiences we hold onto over our lifetimes. We are not taught as women the power of these portals and we see the effects of this out in the world. Our wombs then become like storage spaces rather than the vortexes and uncluttered spaces that they are meant to be and our pussies become dry portals lacking juice for our creative endeavours.

This four-step cleansing practice[*] can be used to build our relationship with our bodies and know them on a deeper level.

---

[*] This practice is inspired by my time training with my teacher Dr Shakti Malan.

- Write a short letter to every past lover that is still in the field of your sexual energy portals. Honour them, thank them, and express what you need to. Then, ritually throw all the letters into the fire or bury them in the ground, speak the words out to the wind or the sea. Let the elements be your ally as you release each lover energetically. As you do so, say: "I release you (the person's name) from my inner sacred space." Or words that feel aligned with you.

- Identify three ways in which you have used your body sexually. Examples could be: stress relief, to lift your mood or that of your partner, as a means to get something, out of boredom… Bring awareness to how you may use sex as an impulse to cover something else and make a commitment to gently guide yourself away from that behaviour.

- Write down in your journal or have a conversation with a friend about your relationship with 'performing' in bed. Do you feel that you have to perform in any way? If so, how? What are your patterns of behaviour around this? How can you start to let these go? How would you like to be in bed?

- Reflect on the ways you have become distracted whilst engaging in sexual intimacy. In what ways do you avoid being present, stop your feelings, leave your body, focus on your partner's experience and not your own? Which if any of these patterns are you willing to let go of?

Just engaging with and reading these questions can activate a clearing process. Be gentle with yourself and seek assistance if needed.

MY STORY

I starved myself from so many forms of true connection, including picking unavailable men: a pattern learnt from watching my parents' relationship play out. I favoured lack rather than abundance. I left myself depleted and had nothing to give those dear to me. Now, I can feel all the places where my own lack of nourishing and mothering myself had an impact on those that followed in my footsteps.

I believe I was given a gift from the universe to demonstrate exactly this and the power of a woman's body when she connects with strong intention to the healing of her relationships and the clearing of her womb space.

Our wombs are so powerful and I got to see my own medicine in flow. After completing an energetic clearing of my womb space similar to the one above, which included the removal of the energetic of ex-partners and friendships that I thought could be lingering as attachments in my energy field, the universe aligned the path of my most recent current ex-partner to cross with my own. Within minutes he turned up out of the blue. He found me walking on the beach. Considering I had recently turned him away from my home, I was surprised that he approached me. But I could tell that there was something different about his energy as he walked up to me.

He had an air of strength about him. And I felt love flowing from him. He approached me with such directness that I immediately opened to listen. He spoke of his deep love for me on a soul level and the mistakes he had made in our relationship for it to break. There was no blame, no games, no needing anything back from me, there was just pure love there. It felt like a fantastical extension of the womb clearing that I had done earlier was rippling through time and space. I felt it energetically moving through our ancestry. I felt the dissolving of our deeper mother and father wounding. For that short period of time, we were both spanning timelines and in an alternate reality.

This was a beautiful completion to a relationship that to the outside looked out of synch. And on some level, it was. We were never going to be life partners. From a personality perspective he was so wrong for me. But on a soul level he was the perfect counterpart to trigger my deepest awareness of the outdated patterns I still held. He was an ordinary 9-5 guy who had no inkling of who I truly was or what I did as a sacred sexual priestess. His life, like mine before, was so mapped out – school, college, work, marriage, kids, retirement, death. Nothing more and nothing less. For him to meet a free spirit like me was a revelation to his ordered life, and opened his world in so many ways.

And for someone like me, who through her own wounding hid and dumbed her power down when it came to men when in relationships, our coupling was a perfect match. I could play small and feel safe and not take full responsibility for the gifts that I carried. We played our roles well, both of us trying to fit into some narrow narrative of what a relationship 'should' be. Both speaking a different language to one another. Yet on an intimate level we were perfectly aligned, for a while anyways.

On some level our connection felt like a win-win. Yet, the only path it would really take would be to inevitably implode because our frequencies were becoming too far apart…and each of us was too out of each other's range of understanding and one another's values in the world. Our connection was soulful to say the least. I will always have love for him. He was a great teacher. We were perfect for each other's soul growth and soul evolution. He wasn't a man of many words when it came to emotions. He, like many men, had been conditioned to see that emotional expression was weakness. We helped one another see multiple faces of the feminine and masculine currently at play in the world through our interactions with one another. All the places where balance was needed. I know for him to turn up in that way, open-hearted, expressive and open in his full masculine presence was a testament to how much healing can actually happen when we enter into relationships as women aware of their sacredness.

My ex-partner didn't come to say anything other than what he needed to. It was as if he knew and could feel the healing that had taken place in my body and he came to complete the process in that exact moment. And then he left as quickly as he showed up. I saw him walk away as a compassionate warrior. I got to see that through our time together he got to taste a flavour of the feminine long-forgotten. He got to feel the Mother essence without being mothered. This eventually led him to a remembrance of the higher more divine fragments of the feminine and the masculine within himself. He got to feel more complete and so did I.

*

I do believe that we as women play a vital role in the healing of the split between the masculine and feminine. If we are the ones with more awareness, then it is up to us to guide the flow of its trajectory. And this isn't saying that we do all the work in relationships. Yet, there is something in the power of our bodies and wombs that can hold the alignment for union to take place on many levels.

I have learnt to have so much compassion for our men who are stuck in the distorted paradigm of patriarchy, who ultimately are only taught that the feminine is there for their gain. I have learnt to feel his deep longing to be connected and plugged back into Her and his inability to do so because of deep conditioning. And I got to see how ultimately holding the line of the exalted feminine can bring our men into full alignment, when we as women stand centred and align to the core power portals within our bodies without wavering or falling into devaluing the power we hold. This is the key to rebalancing the masculine and feminine energies within us. In this extractive paradigm we get to learn not to take from one another as the old programming dictates. We get to learn how to love without judgement.

Our healing doesn't have to be complicated. It can happen in an instant when we set a strong intention. We never fully know why someone has been sent our way, especially if we come at the connection from our mind's perspective. Our souls always know the way and will lead us to the perfect meeting of another soul, to bring to completion to a pattern that may have been running through lifetimes. Until we take full responsibility for the part we play in our distortions, the fractures will remain in place.

So many of us at this time have come for that very reason: to mend the cracks that have appeared in our ancestral history in relation to our relationship trauma. So much of our wounding was created in connection with another, and so much of it can only be undone in relationship with another. Whether that's with an intimate partner, a child or a friend, it really doesn't matter: it is all about the soul. We are the misfits that never fit into our families, and we were never meant to. We came with a specific purpose, specific skills and specific time locks within our DNA that get activated at the right time to shift our whole family lineage to a new timeline.

Womb

All life is incubated in the portal of the womb, yet we treat both the womb and the woman as though they are insignificant to life. We have lost the true nature of what it is to birth souls into this realm of creation. We have forgotten what it is to embody the Mother as mothers. We have lost the spiritual nature of birth both literally and metaphysically. Our wombs are the portals through which souls are brought to this plane of existence from another dimension. Just breathe the reality of that in: we are the portals to other worlds.

We seem to forget that without Woman there would be no life. Yet women have relegated themselves to mere shadows of their understanding of the miraculous portal that brings to life creation. When we are out of balance with our true nature all life around us also becomes misaligned. Our erotic energy is the fabric of life. It is the pulse of life. Yet it has been shrouded in shame. It has become one of the most distorted energies on the planet: misused and abused and treated as a commodity. There is still a lot of soul reclamation that needs to take place from the clutches of shame when it comes to our sexual life force.

In stripping away the holy nature of our bodies we have bought into a medicalised version of them. The body of Woman has been split into parts and the energetics of the womb-space is not seen as whole, but instead as a mechanical thing, the eggs, ovaries, womb, cervix all separated and reduced solely to their reproductive purpose. We view the entry point of our bodies and receptivity – our pussy – with little or no reverence for its holy nature as the gateway to our inner temple. It has direct connection with the opening of the heart and the opening of the voice in women. The connection between vulva and voice is an important one to note when it comes to women being fully in their bodies and connected to their intuition. On a physical level, the anatomy of the voice box and the internal hammock of the body – the internal anatomy on which the vulva sits – are almost identical in their structure and their tissue matter. On an energetical level, when we as women close down either our voices or our vaginal potency, we have the potential of affecting one through the closing of the other.

When we don't use our voices, we cut off the flow of our vital life force that comes up through the body. And when we are closed in our sexual potency, we may find it hard to connect to and voice our deeper feminine wisdom. Between these magical portals are the womb and the heart which are also intrinsically connected and work in a pairing. When we as women connect deeply to these four centres – throat, heart, womb, and pussy we are able to be more in flow. Without this, it's like having a car with no fuel, or no engine. Each component has a role to play in opening to our full feminine potency.

*

Over the past few years, we have seen the last pretence of respect for the birth-giving woman disappear. The vitality of a mother's nurturance is beginning to be erased with the notion of artificial wombs on the horizon. We read headlines that speak to the womb being used as an incubating space, the potential for women in vegetative comas to be used as surrogates. The lack of consent is astounding. The lack of soul awareness even more so. This kind of blindness is so often seen as medical advancement, when it is so far from it. It is a disembodied understanding of the portal that is the womb, narrowing it down to just biology. In my eyes this is one step too far in our push forward for advancement. It is the continued erasure of the sacredness of Mother in all Her forms.

This is not something new, it has been going on for millennia, it has just shifted form and taken on a more sophisticated narrative. Which isn't always easy to recognise because we have become used to scientific breakthroughs as being the dominant description of our world. Science and academia have become the only measuring sticks for information when truth isn't always a tangible thing.

*

The power within the womb often lies dormant, detached from its mystical web: a force so misunderstood by the masculine way of being that values freedom and non-attachment. Longing, when fully felt, activates the womb and begins the manifestation process of our deepest desires. Yet, how many dare to tread its watery depths and feel its pulsating song, one that opens and activates the womb's magnetic capabilities to manifest?

Acknowledging pussy as portal and womb as temple is a reminder that this is the seat of your power and has gifts to give you, way beyond sexual activity. Through them you are taken into the realm of conscious awareness, into the depths of the body. To know them is to know Her beyond the intellectual. To know Her is the path of reverence, remembrance, sensation and embodied being. We have been cut off from Her and from our sacred female bodies for way too long. It is time to come home to yourself.

MY STORY

Sometimes being a mystic is unpredictable and challenging. I have had visions and visceral sensations of the full spectrum of the collective harm done to women. It happened once during a routine smear test which was quite rough. The moment my cervix was touched, I was transported back along the timelines to my own trauma wounding and then further back in time along the timeline of harm caused to all women.

That experience threw me into a deep-freeze trauma response. But when we heal for the collective, the universe always sends the help we need. I received a phone call shortly after out of the blue from a sister friend. And I was going to fall into an old pattern of saying I was fine or that I could sort this out myself. Yet in that moment I knew this was bigger than me and I had to surrender to the overwhelm. In that moment I was held and witnessed as I cried and felt the full gravitas of being thrown into a collective imprint of trauma.

EXERCISE

PUSSY PORTAL CONNECTION

I highly recommend you create a practice of connecting with the portal of your pussy daily. The pussy prayer below has been adapted from the work of Jaiyé, creatrix of Black Girl Bliss and the work in her book *Pussy Prayers*. You don't have to say the full prayer daily but an acknowledgement that you recognise her power and presence is a good way to keep your awareness of your relationship to her.

> *I lay one hand upon my pussy and one on my heart and say: I declare my pussy is eternally blessed, loved, creative and healed. I release all physical, mental, emotional and spiritual pain and trauma experienced in this lifetime and all previous lifetimes. I dismantle and alchemise all emotional and psychological fragments projected by others. I unhook and unbind myself from all previous lovers. I affirm my pussy as my own creative and sacred-pleasure centre, a gateway to the divine. A portal to the realm of the original creation blueprint and organic life. My pussy belongs to me. My sensuality guides me. My sexuality is fully centred at the seat of the core of my being. I am sovereign within my body. I am free to explore the depth of my power. I am free to express the breadth of my passion. I am free to embrace the full range of pleasure through my body and my pussy. I attract to me joyful and sacred connections rooted in love and respect. I honour and revere my body as a sacred vessel. I declare it so, and so it is!*

Additionally, here is a Declaration of Devotion to your womb that I have adapted from the work of Thema Azize Serwa, founder of Womb Sauna, as an alternative to be used in conjunction with or alone as you build a deeper relationship to your womanly body parts:

My dearest womb, you are the centre of my being, the centre of all life. You are the inner sanctum that connects me into the field of the Mother's womb and reconnects me back into her restorative light. As I do so, I realign with the deep wisdom that resides within. I remember you as the sacred space that you are. I acknowledge that my creative power is the same that springs forth from the wellspring of life. And I declare myself to be a reflection of that creative force as I rewrite our story.

You may not always have been honoured with dignity. At times you have been treated with disrespect, discounted and even traumatised. I know there have been times when I was unable to control what happened to you. Today, as I allow the healing waters of the Mother to flow through, together we wash away all distortions and release past hurts from our temple walls and anchor into her original codes. From this point forward I affirm that our relationship will change as I take time to listen as you ask for your voice to be heard and restored to its rightful status. You are the missing piece of the puzzle of my life. Together we craft a more aligned story, both for myself and for the collective field of womanhood. Together we weave a new world into reality as we lean into the mystery. I declare to take care of you with the reverence you require. I am grateful for our journey together; you are my sacred seat. I trust your power on a deeper level as we enter this new terrain of being a woman embodied in her full essence. I give thanks for all the wisdom you hold. I love you.

Note what is arising in you. Write it out and begin to have a dialogue with both gateways. They both have a voice, what do they want to say to you? I know if this is new to you, it may be confronting to connect to the deepest part of you in this way. Especially when there may be painful memories that you would more than likely want to forget. Or your experience of being a woman may have been less than favourable. You may have bought into narratives about your body parts being offensive or that they are misshaped in some way and have to be plucked and tucked. Yes, memories will arise, it is inevitable, we live in a world that has so much to say about your genitals. Choose to back yourself, to not abandon what she wants to say to you. Be with the discomfort. Show her some love. Embrace her. Worship her for the magic that she is. Your body knows what to do to move through anything that arises. Trust her and thank her for all that she is, for all that she has served.

Dear Woman,

Know that you can command matter,

Changing the field around you just by connecting deep inside.

Matter equals Mother, equals the material of this realm.

The true template of Woman has been manipulated for thousands of years,

Hijacked and censored in order to keep us from our true power,

From our sexual power, our creative power centre: the womb.

Yet we know that it is the portal to the infinite, a living oracle with its own voice.

A voice that we can harness for humanity at this time.

The womb is a magnificent source of power.

She is and You are an unstoppable force.

Birth

We are innately encoded with the Mother codes in our DNA and when we tune into our deepest biological truth, we know how to give birth. Yet, we have lost the initiations and rites of passage into womanhood that taught us the truth of that. We have lost connection to the body's wisdom and have been infused with and adhere to a medical model of birth that takes us further away from our inner wisdom.

With birth, just like with sex, we have been taught the exact opposite of our body's natural abilities. We have been taught to move fast instead of slow, to create tension not relaxation, contraction not expansion. The word 'contraction' is written into the birthing experience. What would happen if we tuned into another way of knowing that speaks of our ability to spontaneously eject our child during birth?

We are taught that the body contracts when we are giving birth. That the ring of the cervix contracts and that we have to push outwards to have our babies come into the world. This is not accurate. The cervix actually expands upwards around the head of the baby. But in a world where everything is about outward force, we have come to a consensus that we need to push hard against the opening. We are not given time enough to go with the flow of the body and to let the rising occur naturally. We put birth on a timer. We give it specific goals to reach. So much so that we will induce the mother if we think it is taking too long. It is the same with sex. We do not allow enough time for the body of the woman to get into a natural flow where her tissues engorge and are full of her essence so that she can open naturally. We force the process to the point that a large percentage of women report having uneventful sexual experiences and often have sexual encounters without orgasm. We have been conditioned to believe that an orgasm arises and stays only in the genital area and is again a forcing outward of energy, when in truth, and especially for the woman, her vulva and clitoris are connected to the largest system of nerves through the body and with adequate time and attention we can have full-body orgasmic experiences.

Women require far more time for arousal than we are led to believe. Our bodies work very differently to that of the male body that can become aroused far quicker. In a world where bigger, better, faster has become the norm we have short-changed ourselves and in doing so have lost the art of sex. And we have certainly disconnected our sexual energy from the birthing process which seems a little short-sighted considering it is how babies are created in the first place. If we were to get over this disconnect, the process of birth could be centred around pleasure rather than pain.

It is reported that about 2% of women experience orgasms during birth and about 1% of women experience 'foetal ejection reflex', also known as spontaneous pushing, when the body of the woman expels and releases the baby without force or pushing. The body does what it needs to without any intervention. It happens mostly when the body feels safe to open of its own accord. The fact that we have to create a medical term for this demonstrates how rare it has been that the body of woman does what it is naturally designed to do. This knowledge is not commonplace.

We call these things spontaneous rather than natural because we have been so conditioned away from the female body's natural flow, its openness and receptivity. The energetic pole of the female body is designed to receive, we have openings specifically for that reason. Yet so much is done by force.

We over-complicate most things in the world. We want to innovate, make things more efficient, including the body. Yet when we allow room for opening, for true alignment, the innate life force that is stored in the pelvic region can come into its full capacity, nourishing the flow of the vast nervous system that resides in that area, doing the job it was designed to do, which is to assist in all stages of creating life, from the act of sex to giving birth and beyond without hindrance. We can let the energy stored there move through and nourish the body's tissues.

When we don't give the body enough time to activate its natural sequence, the right hormonal balance cannot come into play and so much of the pleasure hormone oxytocin is not present most of the time during these acts because of the sheer speed of our expectation of how they should happen, and because, in my opinion, they tend to lack reverence and sacredness. Our bodies need to be given enough space and time to be. We need to reorientate back to allowing feminine flow into all processes of birth and sex.

MY STORY

I know my birthing experiences would have been very different if I had known all this. And maybe with this awareness I wouldn't have had to experience my first birth that took me away from my child for the first ten days of her life because I was in so much pain from surgery. Maybe, just maybe, our relationship may have been different.

I bought into the fear about my body when it came to birth. That somehow my body didn't know what to do and that it had to be medicalised in order to give birth.

When my daughter gave birth to her daughter, I remember the story she told me of the raw primal energies that took over when they were on the verge of medical intervention: a deep wisdom arose in her body. A protective fierce mother that let out a resounding "No!" I had no such instinct when I became a mother for the first time. I followed protocol and surrendered the knowing of my body because of fear and just because I didn't know there was another way. I followed what was passed down, the path of ignorance, when it came to my own body.

Second time around, after my first over-medicalised birth in which I had a caesarean, I allowed myself to take charge of my deeper knowing, and went against the medical norm that already had me pinned down to have a second caesarean just because I had had one before. Even though I still had fear around the abilities of my own body, on a deeper level I knew that my baby would come when she was ready, and not forced into an illusionary timeframe.

When I see my daughter now in her new-found role as mother, I see how she is plugged into a deeper knowing. A cellular knowing that goes back to the original source of Mother, an ability to know what to do without words. It is a frequency we emit from our being. We can see it in those that live in that constant vibration, like Amma, the hugging saint. One loving embrace from her can rewrite your whole nervous system. This is the essence of Divine Mother embodied and can be cultivated by us all. It is time.

Mothering

We are unable to see a mother as a whole woman. We split her into roles, the mechanics of what she does, thus removing her from what mothering truly is.

Soul and body unite in the body of Woman as she steps over the threshold into motherhood. The portal of the womb becomes activated as a multidimensional stargate to bring through the soul of the child. As a collective we have diminished and minimised this miraculous event. We have narrowed the process of birth down to its mechanical components and it's time to remember that this is divine embodiment in motion. Our culture would have us believe that to be a mother we carry out certain acts, when in fact motherhood is first and foremost an energetic frequency we hold within our bodies. And we carry it whether we birth a physical child or not. The personification of being a mother isn't a doing activity, it is an embodied sense of being.

*

As a collective we have forgotten what the role of mother truly is: guiding a soul into reality and helping them ground into their bodies. This is a role worth its weight in gold, yet we treat mothers with little or no reverence for the enormity of what that actually entails. There is now a growing resurgence of embodied motherhood rising on the planet, born from the desire to find a new way of being, rooted in the understanding that when a mother is fractured this fracture is passed on to the child down the lineage of our ancestors.

There will come a time when we remember that raising a child isn't just the sole responsibility of the parents who gave birth to the child. That the raising of our children is a full societal task. We are the ones who can create a more intimate environment for them. When we embrace the Mother frequency and know that we are all the mothers of the world, here to steward it and each other. A child will become a collective endeavour, raised with its highest potential at a soul level in mind. I first came across this notion in Penny Kellie's book, *Robes*. She speaks of how it will become a group decision as to whether a couple is ready to bring in a soul. They will be seen as the main carers, yet the welfare of all who come into contact with the child will be examined on a physical, mental, spiritual and emotional level. So many of the 'incoming souls' now are children with abilities way beyond that of the current generations and they need extra care and attention. It feels aligned that we will evolve to a place where their welfare is paramount.

*

When we are incubated in our mothers, if they have any fears any doubts about carrying us or being enough for us, we feel those feelings through being inside her. While we are in her waters, we can create what is called a 'nourishment barrier' that can go with us our whole life, according to David Hartman and Diane Zimberoff.* This can have us carrying a strange feeling that we are not wanted on some level or we carry the belief that we were the cause of our mother's stress, somehow responsible for her feelings. We live in a state of deprivation, not really going for what we want or need in life because we feel we can't have it.

Hartman and Zimberoff go on to say that we learn to defend ourselves against taking in the nourishment available to us on a physical and emotional level because our first experience of receiving nourishment made us believe that it came at a price. We learn to tolerate environments lacking in nourishment. This then bleeds out into our later lives as blocks to things that may bring us a sense of fulfilment. We don't go for the career or relationship we long for. We arrange our lives in such a way that a sense of nourishment is never reached.

We are not taught how to receive nurturance and tender care. If we do not trust the feminine it is really hard to receive care and nourishment. The planet is in the state it is now because of a lack of nourishment. We have created under-resourced people because of our lack of honouring of the Mother.

An undernourished mother is an undernourished woman and is an undernourished carer. So many women come into motherhood already depleted. So many women do not want to say that motherhood felt like a burden or hard work. The levels of tiredness that can ensue when we are playing so many roles can be soul-destroying.

Resentment can come when we are taught that we have to let go of who we were before becoming a mother. So many let go of their dreams and desires when they do not need to. The way the world is set up leaves little room for us to explore them freely when our role is solely focused on being mother and not ourselves too.

The uninitiated mother struggles the most because she has to learn everything on her own. How many of us go through womanhood uninitiated, not having our rites of passage through to motherhood? Motherhood then becomes

---

* Hartman and Zimberoff, "The Nourishment Barrier: The Shock Response to Toxic Intimacy"

somewhat of a guessing game because we no longer live in close family units that are multi-generational. We learn from books and logic rather than witnessing lived experience.

We all have access to the Great Mother's energies. It is where we are all returning to on this evolutionary journey: back to the centre of the Cosmic Womb. We do not have to feel deprived or play out scarcity anymore. We can tap into her and receive the nourishment we may never have received from our birth mothers.

MY STORY

We may find ourselves trying to make up for the woman our mother was not. We may overcompensate and want to fill the gaps with who we think she needed to be. Or we may try to push back, so as not to be like her, rather than be the woman that we came to be. I tried so hard not to be my mother, rather than be the mother I was actually designed to be. I didn't give myself the space to actually find out what that was. Instead I constantly searched for the nourishment I thought I missed. It created such a pendulum swing throughout my life. I was never settled as a mother. I carried the demons of my past close. I rejected my true self in their favour. It takes up a lot of energy to not be oneself. Energy that could be utilised for good instead of feeding ghosts. I wasn't able to see myself just as a woman, and I wasn't able to see my mother that way either. This was a ripple that passed down to my eldest daughter. It strained our relationship. She too wanted me to be someone I was not.

My eldest child was definitely one who would have benefited from having a group of people to raise her. She was a big soul from the day she arrived. I never understood that in her, just like my mother never understood that in me. I remember when she was around the age of five, she would come out with things such as, "Why do you not know who you are, mother? Do you not know you are god?" She could see beyond the veil. She was already tapped into the Mother and could see right through me. And I was the same with my own mother.

But adults do not like it when children can see underneath the shadows they hold. Especially when they carry so much trauma and masking: it can be confronting to be seen so clearly through the eyes of the innocent. So much fear has been passed down through our lineage and we have made aberrant rules that shut each other down from a young age. I realise now my mother had unprocessed trauma and I became a mother with unprocessed trauma and did the same thing. I had a dissociated relationship with my body which was passed onto me.

There is often guilt and judgement around being a good enough mother as our human capacities often fall short. We have, as a collective, put so much pressure on the capabilities of mother, putting the good mother on a pedestal. We fall into the trap of trying to do all things alone.

It has taken many years and the removal of many layers of disempowering beliefs to release the archetype of 'mother as martyr' from my body. I never knew that it was possible to mother without feeling guilt or shame, and there are still remnants of that within, and the over-giver in me can raise its head in subtle ways.

At the time of becoming a mother, I did not question who I would need to be. A woman who would be fully able to put the needs of another before her own. A woman with a regulated nervous system. A woman who would not collapse at the first sign of hardship. I just knew I wanted a child: I wanted something to love like I wasn't. I was self-focused. I gave no real thought beyond birthing my child. I had a belief that I could do it all. But I couldn't. I was so dysregulated, yet had no words for that. The closest understanding that was given to me was the possibility of post-natal depression that would pass. But that wasn't it. I was someone who had unprocessed trauma that would play out as my role as mother grew.

Wanting motherhood to be a certain way will never bring any form of satisfaction. You will always want it to be more or less in some way, to be different because we have been sold a fantasy for so long. We have plastered over the truth of motherhood with unrealistic expectations. So much of our consideration of what it means to bring a child into this world is on a limited bandwidth. It comes so much from our personal need, rather than the consideration of whether we are fully able to be with the soul that wants to come and experience Earth at this time. I know for me this was an afterthought. I was in no way ready to have a child. Had I known about the effects of passing on trauma epigenetically, I know I would have given it more thought. I would have done the work to clear the way for the incoming soul to have a smoother ride.

If I had understood my role as a mother was to be able to regulate a child's nervous system, I don't think I would have wanted children until I had learnt how to do that myself. Our children are birthed with a lot of free space for us to imprint with our own coding and beliefs. They may be birthed with much of their personality and primal instincts intact, but on the whole what they learn is shaped by our nurturing them. So much of our task when we enter into being a mother is to foster the development of their innate intelligence, yet because of the way that life is set up, so much of their soul's potential goes into arrested development. I fell into the trap of doing what had been done before in order to fit in. I surrendered my ability to be the creator in form.

Learning to Manage Our Energy

To enter into the realm of the Mother is to learn to hold oneself in full expression without the depletion of our energy. This path is a rite of passage to claim oneself.

We are taught that sensation is bad and so we use much of our creative energy on trying to soothe rather than expand ourselves, to distract rather than focus. Like constantly using your energy for quickies rather than sustainable charge. We have to start seeing our creative and sexual energy as a divine resource that can be used to serve humanity. How would you like to serve life with your precious energy? Are you just using your sexual energy to scratch an itch or to dive deep into the wellspring of life? Are you afraid to hold the force of creation in your body? Do you do things such as overtalking, overeating or over-indulging in activity just to offload accumulated energy? Are you always in rescuer mode, focusing your energy outside of yourself? What do you do to extract or dump energy? The question then becomes: if your energy is a resource, are you serving it well?

Trust your body. It is wise and knows what to do. Just like when we are babies, no one tells us when it is time to crawl or when to start making sounds. It is automatically set on a biological timer already imprinted and encoded in our DNA. This isn't about being taught anything new. It is about using your senses to align with the language of your body and utilising your own universal plugin to Her.

We do not have to strive here. We are resting back into the Mother, a field of consciousness that has always been here, waiting for us to remember and feel the frequency alignment of our original organic blueprint within ourselves. Our resonance with the natural world has a big part to play here too, as we listen to Her whispers rising up through the land. We are choosing what to align with. We are riding the wave of Her current and in doing so we are in service to life.

When women stand in their true essence, we reconnect back to this original blueprint of the Mother, something we have been trained away from. And to do so we require an understanding of the flow of our individual sexual energy. One that fosters a sense of safety and staves off the enslavement of this most potent essence. There is a reason why it is coveted so intensely. It is the energy that creates life and depending on the way it is channelled can be used for restorative or destructive intent. Our role is to learn how to serve it well, and in doing so we create a reality in which we thrive instead of just survive. Our intention is a powerful incantation.

When we realise that we are not separate from life but part of the fabric of it, of something far larger than we can currently comprehend, then how we use our energy becomes an obvious choice. All true connection starts from within. You are a spirit body with a unique frequency. And when you align with that you allow the universal forces to find you and make contact. Like a tuning fork you resound out into the world and let life know you are open for connection.

MY STORY

Safety has been a big issue in my life. I don't remember a time when I ever felt safe throughout my childhood. I had no safe haven to rest in. To create any kind of safety I had to manipulate myself to fit what others needed me to be. I had no idea who I was as a young adult. As an abused child you learn that your body and being are not your own. You belong nowhere except in the mind of the abuser. You become their property to be used at their will. You learn very young to stop living from your innate self and become a chameleon to stay safe. The writing of this book has been a journey into becoming safe in my own skin. It is Her desire that through these words you become safe in your own skin too.

For me, the wounding I experienced played a part in my resurrection and rising. Like Chiron, the wounded healer, the things that terrified and pained me were the things I alchemised and used as my gift to help others remember the potency of who they are. It has been a lifelong journey to accept this part of myself. Working with the essence of the Mother and with the portal of pussy can be quite confronting to some, the two do not seem to marry up. As a society we have sterilised the Mother and stripped her of her sexuality. Bringing that awareness back alive has been the grit in the shell of my life, that eventually created pearls.

Feminine Flow

The language of the feminine is a lost art you have to build your capacity to attune to. The Mother is creating a new lexicon to awaken a sleeping world. Without knowing the language of the feminine, we can begin to believe there is something wrong with us. We live in a world that loves to pathologise, especially when it comes to the nervous systems of women. The lack of awareness of how the female system and body really need to move in this world is very limited.

At times you will question your own sanity as you morph into something never seen before. There will be times when you need to howl as you unravel and release the grief of living a life too small. Know there is no map, you are on the path of faith and trust. Put one foot in front of the other and become a follower of no one. Become your own guru. No one else knows what you are here to do. This is the path of your medicine.

The art of the feminine is to sit with the unknown so we can move to the depths of our being that reverberates deep down in our bones. We are here to learn to wield our power in such a way that means nothing can penetrate us beyond our will.

The world needs women willing to break the norm. Willing to speak from heart and pussy. Willing to stand in the truth of who they are, even if that means standing alone so we can birth something new for the collective whole from our deepest longing.

These are all qualities that have traditionally been seen as feminine within patriarchal culture and therefore disparaged and devalued. How can we embody and reclaim them?

As we have learnt, the way we get into the flow and field of the feminine is through our embodiment. When we enter through our bodies we begin to reconnect back to the sacredness of life.

Our world operates on an over-developed masculine premise that loves to know, grasp, fix, understand, use logic, be in the mind. There is nothing wrong with being orientated out in the world in a masculine way. However, in our current reality we have become so heavily reliant upon it that we have created severe imbalance. Both the masculine and feminine ways are valid, yet we are over-developed in one and under-developed in the other. The realm of the Mother, which is governed by the deep feminine current of life, is a whole different realm of existence to the one we live by now. It is the nourishment that we have been seeking.

We have created so much of a disconnect from the body of us and the body of Earth that we are now in an existential crisis in relation to the natural world. We are disconnected from the current and flow of the Mother. We hunger for Her, yet the only way we know to try and seek Her is through our old over-developed masculine ways of reaching for, doing and trying to control. She cannot and will not be reached that way, so we have to develop a new way of being with life in order to come into contact with Her.

It is through our embodied being that She rises to meet us. There is nothing for us to do but to rest back into the moment, into being received by Her. When we learn to reorientate ourselves in this way, She rises up to meet us. We have to learn to drop our need to perform or to always be in outward action. She is not a commodity to obtain. She is waiting for us to make contact with Her.

We have become under-developed in the language of the feminine. We have lost contact with it because of the way we inhabit our bodies and operate out in the world. We have been missing our direct experience of the magic and mystery that flows through all of life. The current that is the Mother. The flow of life that allows us direct experience of our own sacredness and wholeness. As we come into contact with Her, we realise we are home. And with that, we get to feel our wholeness not as a belief but as a knowing. She, the power that moves through all of creation, also moves through us.

EXERCISE

MINI BREATHWORK PRACTICES TO CONNECT TO THE FEMININE

The breath is one of the simplest ways to connect with the feminine. It allows us to get present with the now, to slow our bodies and minds down and enter the Mother's realm. These are a selection of my favourite breathwork practices. They are gentle, simple and can be done wherever you are. They are influenced and inspired by years of training in the tantra and embodiment field and work with my teachers Dr Shakti Malan, Juliet Gaia and my training as a spiritual healer and reiki practitioner.

BREATHING IN THE REALM OF THE MOTHER

- Take a 5-minute walk. As you do, take a deep breath in through the feet and then exhale out through the feet, knowing that you are breathing in and out in connection with the Earth. Allow the sensation that you are breathing in nutrients of the dark rich soil into your awareness.
- Then bring that breath into the pelvis and exhale from the pelvis.
- Then breathe into the heart, exhale through the heart. Centre in your being.
- Now imagine that your feet have the capacity to fully listen as you walk along the ground, and that as the information rises from the Earth you fall into a place of deep listening as your feet receive and hear the incoming intelligence.
- Allow this to extend through the whole of the body which is now filled with the quality of deep listening. The whole of your being is receiving.
- Let your mind know that it doesn't need to know anything – your whole being is taking in and translating the information it is receiving into its own language.

BEING WITH THE MOMENT

- Take 5 minutes to be still and with the moment. There is nowhere for you to go, you are resting back in the body and just noticing the moment.
- Start to become aware that time isn't just a linear thing that moves in one direction only.

- Imagine it being able to reach in and down. Take your awareness inward and allow time to appear to slow down.

BE THE HOLLOW FLUTE

One of the previous breathing exercises earlier in the book focused on the central column that runs through your torso just in front of the spine.

- Bring your awareness back to this place. This time imagine it to be a pillar of light that holds a level of stillness that is beyond any kind of stillness you have felt before. It is so still that not even your breath flowing in and out disturbs it. It was there long before you even knew it to be there and will be there ever more.

- Just breathe and be with the stillness for 5 minutes.

THE INTIMACY OF YOUR SURROUNDINGS

- Have the awareness as you breathe that you are not watching the breath, rather, you are the breath.
- Allow yourself to feel everything around and within you as the air pours into you.
- Allow the air to fill all of you as you breathe all the way in and out.
- As you do so, bring your awareness to the back of the body and allow yourself to have the sensation of your eyes resting back in the head.
- After a few minutes open your eyes and hold your gaze on one object.
- Let the image of the object come to you instead of projecting out to see it. Switch the orientation of your gaze from one of projection to receivership.

YOUR WHOLE BODY AS AN OPENING

- Imagine all the pores of your body are listening to your surroundings.
- Feel the skin of your whole body begin to have its tiny pores open more as tiny breathing portals.
- Let every single one open as you take in the energy field around you.
- As you breathe in your surroundings through your skin, open your eyes

and look around your environment with a sense of awe and fascination as if seeing it for the first time.

An End to Struggle

After spending many years digging around in the shadows I was so ready to find another way to alchemise the pain. Don't get me wrong, spending some time in the shadow doing the work to clear ancestral imprints has value, yet I think in a world that has spent so much time in trauma, we have got stuck in the digging in the dirt and now it's time to tend gently to the soul. I feel it is time for a switch up for those that have been doing the work of soul searching and working hard to gain achievement to move into a different way of being. We are ready for a new evolutionary edge of growth. We are leading humanity to the lighter side of alchemy. We do not have to be so immersed in the depths anymore: the Mother World can help us align to a more nurturing way of tending to our personal growth.

Many of us have chosen a very hard way of being in collaboration with life. The narrative that we had a harsh punishing god didn't help. But we can now choose to not be so hard on ourselves as a collective – we can tend to the harsh voice of the masculine paradigm and find out what is driving this within us and outside of us. Internalised misogyny often just wants love and attention. We have spent centuries clearing out the dross and now we can exit the karmic looping, repeating the same stories. We can put down the barriers and the shields, we can learn to lean into our vulnerability.

We can begin to see that there is a lighter frequency, a more subtle realm of awareness available to us. A realm that, when we connect to it and rest back, we can open to our own higher aspects of consciousness. We can, from this different perspective, begin to see our challenges as opportunities that aid us in gaining clarity of where we need to tread next on the path.

We can stop digging in the trenches of our lives. We get to a point on the journey where to do that is no longer in service to our soul. We get to a point where we have to say we are willing to let that go and trust that we can go internal and listen to the voice of the soul and be led in faith and trust. It's a place on the journey where we let go of the drama and the notion that we have to earn our healing, or work really hard at it to validate seeing miracles or good in our lives. When, in fact, both miracles and a stream of goodness happen spontaneously in our lives.

In our current time we have got so used to this part of our collective human story of density, heaviness and destruction that we see this as how we are supposed to live. Yet deep down we feel the unease that all is not well and that things are severely out of alignment. We can truly tap into lighter fields that are all around us and see life through a completely different lens, one where we are not carrying so much extra baggage from our ancestral history and past. We can ask to put it down, to let go of the burden and connect to a different version of ourselves and life.

We just haven't got the memo on a larger scale yet that this is a possibility. We are at a level of our evolution where we can open up to more, where the possibilities of a radically different new way are totally plausible. Life is changing so rapidly and our conscious awareness of a lighter more aligned field that we can tap into and operate from is growing. We can get to see that life can be easeful and joy-filled. We get to be in the present time and hold the tension between where we are now and the future trajectory we are bringing into being. By seeing this as an unfolding that can happen naturally, we get to let ourselves off the hook of thinking this is some sort of big effort-ing mission. We instead get to turn inwards, soften, slow down and listen for the next right step through our intuition.

We get to know that making mistakes is part of the process. That surrendering ways we operated in the past and related to the world can be messy. The only way to know Her is to feel Her and trust and believe that She is there always.

MY STORY

We are learning to connect to the unseen and follow the internal nudges.

I got to do just that. I got to say to myself that I am going to trust in this energy, this force that descended down on me, around me and in me. This Mother essence that had no judgement, only love to give. When you get to a point in your life where you feel the only option is to take your life because you feel you have nothing tangible to believe in anymore, then you have got nothing to lose. When you are led to follow the unseen and trust that it is there for your highest good, it stops the endless searching for something outside of yourself and brings you into a focused clear vision.

The key to that was to follow the sensations in my body. To get good at knowing what a strong 'yes' and a strong 'no' feel like in my body. And be free enough to say no to anything that didn't feel right, not just going with the flow.

We get to follow the truth of what we are here to create in the world by truly listening to what wants to flow from the core of us, rather than being stuck in perpetual outward searching. Moving forward, you get to create from a place that knows the whole of you. And that may mean doing things that don't make logical sense to your human mind and facing aspects of yourself that come up to be embraced from the shadows. I got to see all the layers of truth in relation to my story, and all the places where I got things wrong which enabled me to see the bigger patterns at play when it came to the mother wound. Because of that, I got to know my gifts and heal ancestral imprints. You get to see that you create and define the meaning of your life and how you are going to show up for it.

The realm of the soul and that of the Mother are places that have a lot of clarity in them. And with that we don't have to figure out how to get there, the process of moving forward from that directive is the thing that builds the world we want to see out before us.

Embodying Her

Mystical woman, now is the time to embody your rightful place. You are here to create a new edge of human potential that no longer follows the static rules of life. No more imploding or exploding, you can develop the capacity to hold more of who you are. You not only have the right to exist, it is essential that you do. Learning to love who you are now without having to change a thing is the greatest gift you can give to yourself. Sit with kindness with your own inner struggles. Get up close and personal with your wounding, your internalised fear, so that you can begin the process of mothering them back into being. The daughters of the world that come after us need us to shed light on the mysteries of the feminine. We can be the light that guides them to know what lies behind the veil.

We must honour our biology as the shifts intensify and more of our awareness gets switched online. Learning to sense, to feel the body is essential. Using the gift of our sensitivity is key. If we do not integrate, then we break.

I know so many of you have not felt like Earth is home, yet know that if you are here there is a reason for this. If these words reach you, it's because you feel a resonance in your being. You are beginning to attune to a new paradigm and separate yourself from the old one before getting swept out to sea with it. You are beginning to listen to the deeper call of your soul. In the old paradigm you felt like you didn't belong. Also, maybe like I did, you felt like you didn't want to be here at all.

Yet, the time for dissociating from the sacredness of the Mother is over. It is a holy act of service, a sacred duty to reconnect to the portal through which all mothers are made, whether you are or desire to be a mother that births a child or not. The reclamation of pussy is a revolutionary act. We are removing the clutches of her monopolisation by the medicalised institutions. We are freeing her overtly sexualised, objectified and vilified labels.

We are remembering that she is the portal of all new life. She is power. She is your solid base. Without her, you do not have a full navigational map to your innate power. Your relationship to her sets the scene. As Woman you have the ability to change the environment around you just by being present to your sacred seat. When heart, pussy, womb and throat are in full alignment we begin to regulate our nervous systems and with that we can command and set the tone of a room. We have the choice to ripple out into our spaces with radiant being through being connected to the seat of our feminine power.

Do not divert your eyes from the truth of your feminine vessel. She is your initiation into womanhood. Loosen the patriarchal grip from between your legs. Claim her rebellion. Your sacred activism. She will keep you honest. The Mother is asking for our uprising to be birthed through our very being. When we know the richness of our being, we know the riches of the Earth. The power of our pussy is always waiting for our loving embrace: to accept her in all of her glory as the portal of life.

*

We are shifting from healing being an individual endeavour. We recognise that we cannot fully heal alone. Our distortions are so often created through relationship and this is the place that we need to unravel them in. We are here to be in service to one another. And in our connection to one another, we begin to realise that by simply seeing one another for the truth of who we are, the healing naturally happens.

I thought that I needed to punish or deplete myself to in order to serve Her. But living in service to Her does not mean sacrifice. Service can be extremely life-giving. When we feed life, She feeds us. We no longer have to be part of the current reality. We finally get to come off the ride of masculine force and be in more flow. We get to set the tone of how life flows through us. We get to initiate a new way of being: one that is more in alignment with our true feminine nature.

To be in service to Her, we need to let go of the notion that it will somehow make us 'good people'. This is just an extended thread of the 'good girl' and will not work when we are in service to the Mother. She does not need our infantilised identities. When and if we say 'yes' to Her, She will create situations for that to be removed from our psyche. She requires us to be willing to reclaim the whole of our womanly essence to serve. When we serve Her, we serve life.

*

We have to remember that we will not always feel robust in a world so full of toxic distortions. We are moving out of the masculine bravado, that tells us to present as something we are not and sets us up for failure. We are here to show the truth of who are.

Walking the feminine path asks us to be humble in the face of life. It asks us to hold the vision of where we are going whilst simultaneously not fooling ourselves that we are there yet: to be here right now in the present moment at the size that we are and to ask for assistance in our growing. There is a level of responsibility that comes with that, to be aware in the moment of what resources we need so we can grow into our vision, both collectively and individually. Part of that process entails coming into right relationship with our internal masculine.

We as women can have a harsh internal voice, so wrapped up in the distorted masculine inside of us that gets programmed with internalised misogyny and the demonisation of our own feminine. It keeps us stuck in old stories of ourselves and afraid to own and stand in our power. Just like much of the external world, we can easily miss it because we are not aware of the ways we have internalised such a harsh voice, or that it is playing a role in our inaction because it is running in the background. This voice hinders our ability to connect to our deeper feminine wisdom, and to the Mother.

It is important to the balance of life that we take both the masculine and feminine ways of being and looking at life into account. Yet because we have been out of balance for so long, this next phase of our evolution has to focus on the rising of the feminine current. We cannot have balance until we correct the imbalance. The feminine is asking for us to breathe life back into her. Then, and only then, can we have union. Until She rises through us, and our hearts are fully opened to Her, we will continue to create imbalance because we will forever be looking at life through an overactive, overdeveloped masculine structural lens.

When we tap into Her, balance begins to rise organically. The distorted masculine within and without in all of us must submit to the feminine. This isn't about being less than, but it is about being in reverence to Her and dropping the strategies of control. This is how we meet Her. As much as the distorted masculine doesn't trust Her, he also longs for Her. We have to understand that he also carries wounds of the feminine within. He is afraid of the unknown power of Her, that to him is unpredictable. His consumptive behaviour comes from his persistent search for something deeper. Yet he cannot touch it by seeking. None of us can.

When our focus became outward it was also because we were taught that we needed to look externally for a god outside of us, that was detached from the body. And with that came the concept of awakening that took us even further away from form and matter. When we land back in the body, we come back into contact with the sacredness of it and life becomes our mystery school.

EXERCISE

BALANCE YOUR INNER MASCULINE AND FEMININE

Step 1: Recognising the Voice of the Masculine

As with so many women, the number one thing that stops the awakening of our deeper feminine essence is a historical, internalised, masculine voice running in the recesses of our psyches. A voice that we have inherited through our matriarchal lineage that belongs to a time when women were beginning to find their power out in the world but it was driven to be and act masculine rather than tap into their own unique feminine expression.

The voice often says:

"You don't have time for this touchy-feely stuff, to be gentle or soft, we've got things to do."

"You're being needy."

"Get in touch with your feminine? You want to be weak like your mum and overly emotional too?"

"You want to connect to your life mission? We're much too busy."

"Don't even try this. You don't have the strength to do anything of real value You know you're going to fail. All your relationships fail."

The first step to recognising the voice is to acknowledge it consciously without needing to do anything with it. This isn't about making yourself feel bad, shameful, guilty or trying to fix it.

Step 2: Notice How this Voice Runs You

I'm sure many of you can recognise some iteration of this voice. It is part of an outdated version of the masculine that we have internalised that believes in outward performance, achievement and competition.

Be honest with yourself, observe how much is this voice running aspects of your life. It's okay, we have all had this voice dictating areas of our lives. It's a pesky little sucker that has had a tight hold on our being.

Now, with this growing conscious awareness of how this voice shows up in you, you can now engage with it in a conscious way.

Step 3: Have a Conversation with Your Masculine

It is time to have a conversation with this internal masculine voice in you. Here's how:

- Put out three pillows in a triangular shape facing each other. One pillow is 'your' pillow as the feminine. One is for the masculine voice that keeps playing in the back of your head. And the other is to stand in as an observer that holds the Mother essence. Switch between the first two pillows.

- When you are sitting on your pillow, speak to the masculine voice as though you are speaking to a man sitting there. Then switch to the masculine pillow and imagine that you can speak as a man to the feminine. The purpose is to bring more space, awareness and attunement between the two.

- Then move to the third pillow that represents the observer of the two who carries the essence of the Mother and relay back what was spoken between the two.

Here is a suggested flow of the conversations…

- I tell my masculine that I appreciate everything he has achieved up until now. This is important. Without acknowledgment, this masculine voice will not be open to discussing new possibilities.

- I express my desire to awaken to my deeper feminine essence – to feel myself more as a woman, to have more space, to live from authentic impulse, to put my foot on the brakes a little. To open to more softness. Find the words that are true for you. It can be hard for the feminine to ask for what she truly wants, so be gentle with yourself and take your time.

- Then move over to the masculine pillow and let him respond. At this point, he might show resistance and say something like: "You're asking me to change focus. I am really enjoying the success I am having out in the world. This is stupid, what is the goal here?" Again, find the words right for you. Take your time to really sink into your body and feel what wants to be revealed from your core.

- Then go back to the feminine pillow. Now it's time to be appreciative but tactful. Express your faith in the capacity of your inner masculine to take on a new challenge. If this doesn't work, gently make him aware of how exhausting – and how lonely – it is to keep plodding away the way that he has been.

- Go back to the masculine and let him respond. Being made aware of his yearning to have more of the feminine nourishing his space is usually the thing that will have your inner masculine opening and saying yes. Once he's given his support, you are good to go to the final stage.
- Go to the third pillow and sit as the loving benevolent force of the Mother and speak what you need to, to both of them as a unit. Shower them with your love knowing that that love permeates through the whole of your being.
- Record your experience in a journal if you so desire. Or speak it out with a trusted friend or therapist.

(Adapted from my training with Shakti Malan, Sexual Awakening for Women.)

MY STORY

We all enter this life in service to the other. It may not always feel that way because the depth of what some of us go through, the price we pay, feels too high. I often feel that way when I think of my eldest daughter. What price did I have to pay to wake up? I know we come in as sovereign beings and we all have a path to follow, yet to burn through karmic depth that is passed down the line can be a lot to bear. My daughter did me a service. She created enough karmic energy for me to be able to get out of my debt, and I did the same for my mother. The work we do in this life has a ripple effect through all generations, whether they are alive or not.

Our souls come to play different roles and we often do not know what those roles are until we are deep into the relationship with the other soul. And so often those roles go way beyond the labels we give them on a human level. I will always be grateful for the way we, in my maternal lineage, pushed up against one another, even though I often feel I wish it could have been another way. This is not regret. I know, based on who we all were at the time, we did what was necessary in order to be sovereign unto ourselves. I am glad my daughter knew her own mind enough to walk away from what she deemed harmful. Just like I had to do with my own mother. The road of healing the mother wound doesn't always come out smelling of roses on this plane of existence. But in the unseen world I know the ancestors are smiling.

Dear Woman,

It is time to unravel all the places you have felt obligated to play small
To harden. To numb out.
You are the essence of the Mother
You were made for this time. You are a creator seed.
What are the gifts you want to arise from the groundwork you have already created?
Who are the tribe that you are calling in?
We will need community more than ever; it is the way we were designed to be,
No longer the lone wolves, but together in sisterhood and harmony.

CLOSING

EVOLUTION

I can no longer lie to myself
About life,
That all of it is not sacred
And this too is the truth of my essence and being.

So many of us that are highly sensitive are able to feel between worlds and the undercurrent of life. We feel that there is something deeper taking place: a call to awaken, to remember that to live as humans we also have to be in devotion to life. Know that there are many of us that have heard the call. You are not alone. We are the seeds that have been planted in the deep nutrient rich soil of the Mother through which she is rebirthing a new world.

It is time for the medicine and the wisdom of Woman to be fully recognised in the world. For all of the mystery and magical ways to be out in the open. The journey inward that we have explored together here is where we find the language of the feminine. When we share from this place to the world, to our men, what it is really like to be in the body of Woman, we begin to shift the narrative.

We are being awakened out of hibernation mode. The years between 2024 and 2027 are going to be huge activation years. The entire cosmic, planetary, biological and galactic bodies are shifting. A multidimensional shift is taking place. What within you is calling to be heard? What is calling to be loved back into being? What parts of yourself have you neglected? What dreams have you not allowed to pour through into the now? What desires have you let slip away out of your reach and conscious knowing?

Reclaiming the Fierce Feminine

We have had an existence devoid of the Mother for so long. Now the refined frequency that is being poured into and up through the planet is urging us to reconnect back to our original blueprint. The unification of masculine and the feminine plays a big part in this, both internally and externally. The union between heaven and Earth, between matter and soul, between divinity and the mundane. This awakening energy encompasses all the mother archetypes and can be tapped into through the body of Woman.

We have been programmed as a collective away from accepting or even acknowledging one of the key faces of the Mother: the primal fierce mother, the aspect of Her and of ourselves that knows it is here to rock the status quo. We need to summon Her up now.

We have walked on egg shells for way too long, afraid of being shut down for being too wild. Afraid that we will not be met in this place of power, that we will be seen as the 'too much woman'. We are being asked to stand in our pure authenticity: a call from life to rise, to show all the full range of Mother. Stand up and speak your truth, call out the bullshit. Create space in which to howl and bawl out your captive feelings. Let the body tell its tale. Give it space to unthaw the frozen trauma this is locked within. When we release ourselves from captivity, we heal the wounds of the world. When we shift into more of our wild nature, we give permission for others to do the same.

It is no coincidence that my granddaughter had the same untamed wild nature as my eldest daughter had. I can see how I played the game of needing to tame that. I can feel within me where that was done to me. All patterns that need rewiring will show back up somewhere in our ancestral line. They recycle until someone decides to break free from the distortion. I see the places where it was suffocated and squashed, because in both scenarios it was seen as unmanageable and unsightly in some way. My mother's favourite mantra was "Little girls need to sit and look pretty". We see this everywhere in subtle and not so subtle ways: imposed behaviour on our wild feminine chaos that keeps us playing small.

The deeper healing cannot happen as long as we hold onto the expectations of the Mother being some tame thing. When we turn the Mother into a martyr and see Her only value as a resource, we commodify Her and see Her as something to be used. Our whole capitalised and colonised world is built upon this principle.

This is the collective egregore: an energy that feeds off our collective fear. It does not care if it uses you. It does not care if your needs are met. It has no desire to ever let you be whole. Its main premise is to take and take until you have nothing left to give. We see this pattern played out in so many ways. It is the very same pattern that happens in families when you are the one who puts your own needs last, your life force doing all the work. It is the same pattern when we see dominant leaders destroy the world for their egoic gain. It's what we see when we play the self-deprivation game and hide our power. It teaches us to be under-resourced, under-valued and under-nourished, because it teaches us to think of ourselves as separate and consider community as second.

We do not have to be in relationship with the feminine in this extractive way. In fact, when we are, we run the energy the wrong way: it becomes inverted and goes against our nature of receivership. The feminine is a generous and forgiving force. She will give and give until she is exhausted, and then she will slam the door shut. Just like Mother Earth, who makes Her presence known when She unleashes Her formidable force when we push Her too far out of balance. Life is always seeking equilibrium. Ask yourself: "How can I cultivate this force of nature that life wants to stream through me, so that I can hold more of it in my body and for the betterment of all?"

We have been given access to this potent life force energy, but what we do with it is up to us. We have been conditioned to keep its flow stemmed and to build small lives: go to school, go to college, get a job, get a partner, have kids, and then retire and die.

We came here to play a bigger game. We came to be in partnership with Mother Earth and one another, to be an ecosystem that sustains life. There is a level of responsibility that comes with owning this wild energy. It is the reason why so many do not go there. It is bigger than anything we have been taught to be. I have pushed it away myself many times because of that very reason, and instead put the onus on others to make me feel powerful. But when we align with Her that falsehood begins to crumble.

I never wanted to claim myself. The picture I created in my mind of the bigger things that I could do seemed too daunting. I wanted none of that. But in the end, you can't deny who you are and what you are designed to be without consequence. You cannot use life for your own gain without Her pushback.

Dear Woman,

Our new Earth can be a dystopia or utopia – we get to decide.

Astrologically we are being supported to move toward utopia.

To shift from co-dependency to interdependency,

To break up our relationship with unhealthy dynamics

What is it you wish to grow at this time?

What has been rising inside of you to come to life?

What has been asking to have a voice and be heard?

As we move through these times your body is the safest place to be.

This is where you will find the truth of who you are,

The truth that counteracts the long-held agenda to disconnect you from your body.

As shepherding souls, we remind others that there is a reason that they were born in the female form.

We are ushering in the true frequency of the Mother,

She is a wealth of resourceful flow, so come fill your cup.

Remembering

The rising of the Goddess, of Mother, is a pathway into the remembrance of how to be with the body of Woman, and the body of the Earth. Sexual power is the energy that flows through them both. When women remember how much power we have in our bodies, we can begin to turn life around.

In the past, the feminine force took a step back. The time is ripe for it to come back online full throttle. The time for compliance is coming to an end. It had its place, but now it is time for the next level of our incarnation. This isn't about blaming or shaming the past. It is about acceptance that somewhere in our history we relinquished our power for safety. I saw this imbalance of power as I watched the women in my life hand over their power every day. As a collective, we as women became afraid of our power and more so of our bodies. When it came to birth, we became detached from our primal instincts. We were taught at a young age to have disdain for our bodies, for our bleeding, for their function. Holding such judgement against the body throws it out of alignment.

The way we collectively treat the body of Woman is the way we treat the body of Earth. We have little or no reverence for the planet or the body of Woman, both are treated like a commodity, something to rule over or use for gain. We have become steeped in limiting and inverted beliefs that lack any reverence for the feminine. We see this in the way that lack and scarcity play out in the world. We believe the world to be lacking in resources and abundance. When we tap into the feminine realm of life, we see that life is overflowing with vitality.

When men are unable to receive nourishment from the Mother, then they learn to take. In its extreme form this stretches into violence. We see this distortion playing out in a myriad of ways in our current reality, from the plundering of resources, to the number of sexual violations that take place. Each is rooted in a lack of connection to the Mother, to the life-giving element of existence. When we are connected to the Mother it becomes almost impossible to strike out against another being, because we remember that this is the form that gave birth to us. This is the remembrance of the creator and our ability to co-create.

The frequency of Mother is a full spectrum that we can inhabit and embody. It is up to us to show up consistently and committed to serve the energy that calls us. To stay open to life. Even when that means that the things that no longer resonate are shaken up and removed from your life. The feminine can be a path of loss. Relationships and connections that we have tolerated so that we feel like we belong are shaken loose. So often when this begins to happen, people turn away. They think that life is against them, and cannot see the bigger picture of purification. The light that comes through begins to illuminate all the places they have been out of alignment with their true self. We have to trust and have faith that what wants to come is the higher thing.

The Mother helped me to soften the hardness around my heart and bring more love into my world. We are all fractals of the one thing and we are moving into an age where love will dominate in its many forms. It feels far-fetched to say this now, given the state of the world, but I know with conviction that it is true. We will look back at this time with disbelief at how we treated one another, at how much trauma we chose to live with as normal. Now, as we decide to evolve beyond that, and take a leap into a new reality of being, we are getting to see the consequences of our choices. This is a realm of free will and we get to decide what trajectory to take.

Mother World

I am choosing the Mother World. I am choosing the organic world, a world in which we thrive. I am choosing to align with more aligned societies where the thought of creating harm to another seems unthinkable. We can begin to build momentum behind this notion through our collective agreement to choose a world where harm is not at the forefront. We are still at a point where any direction is possible. We are currently seeing both the best and the worst of humanity. We are seeing extremes of polarity. Everything is out on the table.

Whilst held in the deep dark earth of the Mother I was shown a vision of a world where the body of Woman was revered. Where her essence was held sacred and she was safe to own her power, embody her gifts and express her sensuality out in the world. Long before the distortion of trauma and control were imprinted into the psyches of women there was a place where we were fully connected to the Mother on a cellular level. A place where the essence of Woman was free to be its full spectrum self. A place our erotic liberation leads to. We must have faith in our ability to deprogram ourselves from the popular culture that has had us externalise our innate power, and follow the expectations of others. We are co-creating a place where we no longer sacrifice or trade our sensitivity, sexuality or sensuality for a false sense of safety and belonging. A place where we become reacquainted with our existence and reason for being here on Earth now, as we attune to the organic time codes held in the land.

When called to be on a certain piece of land, go. Your very essence maybe the key to unlocking stored pockets of gnosis that need to be brought to light through your vessel. It doesn't have to be more complicated than that. Just being there is enough. Just being is enough. She is calling us through the land. We have experienced so much displacement as a collective people. As we migrated to distant shores over the centuries, we separated from our mother lands. In doing so we lost our sense of self and our relationship with the lands. We became uprooted.

Now we are being asked to plug back in, to ignite the universal wisdom held in the land and to create a grid that spans across all places. I believe we are born in a particular region intentionally. This doesn't have to make any sense to the logical mind. We may have some kind of connection there through our bloodlines or be called somewhere we have no known family ties. We are working on a soul level here, which makes up so much of the foundation of who we are. It knows and feels the erotic pulse of life through the energy of the land and it seeks connection and expression through it.

Being a Force of Nature

Sacred feminine power isn't something we wear or embrace as a new identity or a badge of honour, it is a field of intelligence, a realm of existence that we can rest and surrender into to let it guide us through life. Life wants to hold us in the nourishment of the Divine Mother. She has always been here, waiting for those that hear the call. This feminine frequency radiates out into the world for us to embody as a truth. It is a power that reveres all life. The world is changing, but we have become so arrogant to think that it should always stay the same. Nature is an ever-changing force and so is the feminine. Being Mother, being Woman, is being a force of nature.

This is no time to run off into the woods and escape what is taking place. We came here for a reason. We are here to overcome so many of the limitations imparted to us. We are here to learn how to build capacity in our bodies to hold more of our true essence. And at some point, we have to aid the bringing of the frequency of the Mother out into our world for the future of humanity.

We are slowly being corralled into a reality where disembodiment becomes the norm. The rise of AI and transhumanism is feeding our inability to feel. We are systematically being dumbed down in our sensitivity as our reliance on technology grows. We are being led towards a road of more disembodiment; the transhumanistic movement would have us merge with artificial intelligence in a way that removes our sovereign self and detaches us even more from the functions that make us Woman. As I write this, in the past few days, science has created an 'entity' without the use of either a woman or sperm. A human has been created out of living stem cell technology.[*] There are hopes that they can recreate the human birthing process without the assistance of the female womb. This is a reality that most don't want, but it is one that is facing us. A false matrix has been created where technology is becoming king, ready to take over and take us further away from embodied being. But it requires our consent to participate. This move away from our embodiment has not been an overnight thing. How do you bamboozle a whole species into giving away their power? You turn up the heat slowly over time, like boiling frogs in water.

To fight the system never transforms anything. We have to remember who we are and that we can eat the dark and turn it into endless fuel for our life force. Know that as you burn bright, you are evaporating and disintegrating the darkness that brings about so much disconnection. We have to ask ourselves: How do we want to experience being here on Earth as this era of humanity closes out and we venture into new territory? What new perspective do we wish to embody so we can move in a more harmonious direction? We get to be the living example of the world we wish to see, so that others can make those choices too. As we share information with one another, we become beacons that show others alternative ways of being.

MY STORY...OUR STORY

I know all too well the feeling of living devoid of soul, void of devotion, from cutting myself off from Mother's milk. Lack of letting love in twists the human psyche and turns it into someone that could hurt another soul. It creates the

---

[*] James Gallagher, bbc.co.uk, "Scientists grow whole model of human embryo without sperm or egg," September 6, 2023.

chaos we see out in the world as we stand at this threshold of change. Our collective wake-up call has truly begun. The Mother will not allow us to destroy the planet, even though we may destroy ourselves. This time is asking us to remember the memories of the lineage of the Mother as we collectively dig for Mother's bones. As we learn to be mothered by life and mother for life. For this to happen, we must be courageous enough to face the distortions we created that ripple out in our personal lives, through the mother wounds and our maternal bloodline, to turn the grit of them into pearls of wisdom.

I have lived a life that has taken me to many levels of existence, I have travelled multidimensionally and supernaturally and had the privilege to touch some deeper truths and that has not always been pretty. I know what it means to sit on your creative power, to be afraid to let it be released in the world, until it turns in on oneself and into self-destruction. I had a long history of mental unwellness because I wouldn't allow my energy to pulsate through my being. I would swing between mystical being and being extremely hard to relate to. I was categorised as having bi-polar, my moods swinging from one extreme to another, because I was so emotionally deregulated. What I had was a very large system of energy that I didn't know how to handle.

Fine-tuning to the Mother's wisdom is still a journey I am on. It is one that will be lifelong. As I grow, so does my depth of understanding. I am the accumulation of the life journey I have had. My life is what has created my pearls of wisdom: an embodied knowing that can never be taken from me. All of the suffering has been the key to my gifts. I have never had to do something more painful than search to find the connection to my soul. It has been one of the hardest things I have ever done. There have been so many initiations along the way, I have lost count. You have had snippets of my story here, there is much more to tell. But those are tales for another time. It is enough for now that I finally feel the rekindling of my roots. I finally feel myself belonging to the Earth and belonging to a Mother.

Raising Her Temples

The world has been on the edge of starvation. We have been unable to drink from the well of creation. When the oracular feminine temples were destroyed, we fell into a descent of magnificent proportion. The temples were built over and modern churches put in their place, their energy was syphoned off, and we stopped being able to hear the voice of the Mother. She was replaced with a sky-daddy, and we were told that we had to go through someone else to be in contact with the pulse of life. It was a systematic and multidimensional attack on the feminine way of life.

When they destroyed the Mother's temples it created such a schism in the collective field, such a severance, that many froze in fear and confusion. It created a wounding through all space and time. Humanity has been treading down a path of destruction ever since. Some of us, the sensitive ones, felt those ripples and took the steps to come and clean the house and resurrect what has been forgotten. For many I know it has been a lot to feel the gravitas of it all and choose not to move forward. I know that terror you may feel in your heart. I, too, have felt it, many times over. I know the digging you have to do to get to your truth, to unearth the bones of Mother and breathe life back into them once again. I know the internal darkness you have to face. I know the sting of unfreezing from past hurts. But please know whatever we face, life wants to support you as the ancient codes of the Mother come back to life.

In the Mother World women know and honour their bodies. They know their intrinsic beauty. They know the power of their wombs. They know how to work with the living technology of their bodies. We are each a piece of a larger puzzle. All different for a reason. We are each here to honour our true core essential self. To be the truth of who we came to be.

We are in the process of shifting dimensional realities. Our current reality has a set of fixed rules which we are evolving beyond. Beyond the construct of linear time. Beyond the idea that we are separate from source energy. And embracing more of our divine nature. We are moving into a state where we know that we are creators and we can connect to the living library of the Mother imprinted in our Earth.

We are the trusted keepers of this realm. All the realms throughout the universe have keepers and we are it for this reality. We are here to be custodians of the Earth, living and upholding the covenant of tending to Her wellbeing and also to our own.

We are calling back your power. You get to decide which way you want to go.

Dear Woman,

What do you need to manifest your dreams?

Come suckle from my breast my child,

Come and get the nourishment of the heavens and the nectar of the Earth.

Let me hold and guide you along the way,

Take my hand and let it enfold you,

Take my hand whilst you take your steps into creating your world anew.

Metamorphosis

At this crossroads, both the dark and the light of the Mother have been unleashed. She revealed herself at the time of the Pandemic, a collective activation into the underbelly of life. All the places where we had lost trust in the depths rose up. Life became a threat to our very being. We came face to face with all the trappings we had attached ourselves to. We were shown the true power of nature. We were humbled by the power of Her. She gave us an opportunity to drop to our knees in surrender and drink from the well of creation as we remembered who and what has real power here.

We are at a time in our history when we are remembering that we as human beings have the power and capacity to change our current reality into one that is more fit for human consumption. We are being shown that the death of the old way is not the end of life but a potential beginning. We are being birthed into a new era: one where, as a collective, we are seeking the nourishment of the Mother. We are being called to rise into the next layer of our being, away from the notion of not feeling safe, to embrace all of life.

Our lack of sacredness has led us to a point of no return. In excluding the Mother from the centre of life, we lost the soul of the world. We have swung too far out as a collective from our true nature and now the pendulum is coming back in search of balance. The cycle of life and death cannot be escaped.

We are not transforming alone. The Earth is levelling up right along with us. In fact, it is through Her that we gain access to the new rising frequencies. We are living in times when all the trauma of the Earth is rising to the surface to assist in the evolution and the raising in vibration of the planet into the higher heart. We are moving into a space so that new creativity can spring forth from our loins. We are not being called in ascension out of the body. It is an 'in and down' process of coming into the body to reconnect to our truth and the resurrection of our soul song.

Life is shifting and to some feels like it is dying and falling apart. Yet, just like the dissolution of the caterpillar, whose own immune system attacks itself as its own encoded DNA is set into motion precipitating its own demise, so it may re-emerge as a totally new form. We too are in the activation of new emergence. One that is deeply encoded within. The right conditions are upon us to cultivate our developing evolution by deeply listening. For all metamorphosis to take place, some form of dismantling and chaos is needed.

Evolution never happens in the status quo. We are witnessing the flow of creation in motion, igniting our inherited evolutionary coding. We are being dreamed awake by Her. Pulled deep into the field of Her dark intelligence. Limited internal and external outdated systems accumulated over generations and lifetimes are being stripped back, rewritten and wiped clean, upgrading our soul and human story.

We are switching over circuitry within the body, igniting new ways of living. We are awakening the senses to more receptive states. We are learning surrender and how to be enveloped by the dark. Our old ways of living brought us to this choice point, it was inevitable that what we see now would occur. This is a metamorphic remembrance held deep in the marrow of our bones, here to remind us we are made of stardust and light, dirt and dark. We are awakening our collective memory etched in our cells.

Our Ancient Future

The frequency of the Mother connects us all through Her lineage both backwards and forwards, ancient and new. We have a notion that what we are is a remembrance, yet also know that what comes through has never existed on this planet before. It is a unique combination of all that has been and all that is to come. It is ancient future unity. It is eternal and it comes through each being's own frequency in a combination that we are creating together. Her wisdom was never lost, it was forced underground until this time of reconnection. It has been a necessary part of the journey so we can step into our power of reclamation. If we desire to bring harmony and reverence to life and live in an aligned way with our true nature as humans, then we have to consciously decide to embrace the full essence of the Mother so that She too can come into Her full nature here on the planet as She weaves through all of us. How we embody our beingness has a direct correlation of how She rises on the planet. We are the vessels through which She is landing Her presence here. We must remember that our intention is powerful. And we can co-create a reality in which we thrive rather than just survive.

We as a species have no choice but to evolve. We can do so either with flow or in crisis. We can embrace it with a degree of consciousness or we can be in a state of resistance and make the dismantling process more painful. The feminine is rising and bringing with it many opportunities to embrace a new way of being. One in which we embrace the union of body and soul, where we see the body beyond its physical form and know it as a transmitter of wisdom. Our bodies are living breathing libraries of information and they are waiting to unleash their stored well of gnosis.

Know that the field is ripe for Her more ancient codes to be felt. Over the past years we have alchemised so much as a collective. Now we are shifting into a time of utilising the foundational resourcefulness we cultivated. We are in full revival mode. We are preparing to shift gear. Preparing to build the structure needed for the new Earth matrix, one that includes the Mother equally as much as it does the Father. We have tended the ground, we have planted the seeds, now we are ready to have things grow in union.

Woman, you are both the reminder and the return of Her. You were made for this time of transition. Trained by your life to alchemise the dark and digest it into gold. In doing so you remind your fellow sisters of the new direction and energetic flow. Together, we are the embodied force that can change the course of our planet. Together we are here to speak the language of Mother on Her behalf, and bring Her frequency back onto the planet.

Dear Woman,

We are in a collective soul retrieval,

A revival of the true feminine soul essence

The loss of which caused the closing down of humanity's compassionate heart.

This is our revival. The revival of the sacred codes of Woman.

A remembrance that as Woman, when we are connected

To womb, to pussy, to heart.

We are invincible.

The body of woman is needed.

We are the gateways to other realms.

Through the portal of our wombs, we become a living technology.

Together we are resurrecting the lost codes of the feminine

They are streaming onto and up through the planet.

Know that there are as many ways to express the feminine as there are people.

Not everyone is going to like the messages you bring

But enough will.

In order to bring about a movement of change own your fear and lean into truth and faith,

And together we will resurrect the True Essence of the Mother, because together

We are digging for Mother's bones.

ACKNOWLEDGEMENTS

I am full of gratitude for all the amazing beings without whom this book would never have materialised and been birthed into being.

My dear mama, my muse, the motivation behind the whole thing. In your absence I found the love that always bonds us. This book is an honouring of our journey together in both the seen and unseen worlds.

My children and grandchild Thea, Brogan and Nova, my living legacy. You inspire me to do better and blossom every day. My love for you is limitless.

To the women in my birth family, you are the inspiration for speaking life into our collective story in order to bring healing, insight and deeper love to our maternal lineage.

To my parents without whom I would not be here. It is a gift to be able to use our collective story to bring healing to many as I transformed our woes into wisdom.

Thank you to all the wonderful women I have in my life who have inspired and opened my heart through your nourishing friendship and accountability. Friendships that hold one another to the highest version of one's self and where we can be totally genuine and honest with each another is a gift I deeply treasure.

In particular I hold dear those that have journeyed with me from the very beginning of my healing journey: Jyoti Imix and Carrie Kajda, thank you for being there through thick and thin. You love and see me in ways like no other. Love you, dear soul sisters. Thank you for your presence in my life, I feel held by your love.

And to friends anew who have brought vitality, laughter and community, I honour and appreciate you too.

To all the teachers who saw in me a spark of depth and power even when I could not. The ones that initiated me into being a writer and activated the mystic in me, in particular Siobhan Mac Mahon, Jeanette LeBlanc, Alison Nappi, Jacob Ross and Astara Jane Ashley. Each one of you has been a stepping stone and a guiding light to me holding this book in my hands. I did it, just as you knew I would.

To the teachers who activated my remembrance of the Divine Feminine especially the late Shakti Malan and Juliet Gaia, whose particular flavour of transmitting Her laid the ground upon which I now rest. And to my past teachers who helped me to reframe so much of learning to die to the old and feel the fullness of my soul. Each of you has been a catalyst for me to fly and find my wings.

To the team at Womancraft Publishing, without you this would still be just a stream of words without form. In particular I want to pay my respect to Lucy Pearce, editor extraordinaire, who believed in the book from the very start, when it was just a seed. You never doubted the magnitude and beauty of the book. Thank you all for pouring your hearts into this creation and helping me and it to grow beyond what I had first imagined.

To the cover artist Dorrie Joy. Upon seeing your art, I knew immediately it was the one. It's an honour to have your work on the cover of my book. It is perfect in so many ways.

And of course, where would I be without the unconditional love of The Mother, the divine feminine that flows through all that I do. Your love has held me throughout this whole process and reminded me of why it was important to birth this book into the world. Thank you for revealing yourself to me. I am in devotion and service to your rising.

Last, not least, I thank you, dear beloved readers of this book. I wrote it in honour of you too. If these pages are in your hands, you too have heard Her call.

To all who have experienced trauma, I see you, I hear you.

If you too are drawn to break destructive cycles in your linage, I hear you, I see you. Together we rise. Through the telling of our tales, we raise our voices and guide each other Home. Together we are resurrecting Her bones.

AUTHOR'S NOTE

I began writing this book, or it began writing me, back in 2019 after having a near death experience. I started writing around that time to document what came through me and as a means to mend the past. Then, along the way, I realised that this book was bigger than that: it held threads of a collective story, as well as my own.

It is written as means of making amends and as a call to action for my soul. We all feel and remember our truth differently. This book holds the truth as I remember it and desire to portray it. What is between these pages is written and shared as an act of love. In some sections time has been compressed in honour of narrative cohesion.

I had no desire to be a writer when I was younger. I found most things academic to be a chore. Yet it was the internal drive of my soul that led me to healing many ancestral distortions around illiteracy and the enslavement of our voices and a fear of punishment for using the written word dating back to slavery. Did I know any of that would be part of the unfolding of why I felt compelled to write? No. We don't know until after the fact why we are being guided down a certain path. The call of the soul requires a higher level of trust and faith. We are being guided by something much bigger than us, and our souls have the gifts we need already imprinted.

When the soul calls it really doesn't care about the feelings you may have about what you are here to do in the world. If I had listened to the messages about lacking in intelligence and my lack of focus that I got from school because of my dyslexia, I would never have written this. I would not be here now following a call to bring a message to the world through the written word. I would have been on a very different track. Yet the stirrings of the soul are always there. Even when we do not fully comprehend them, they will rumble in the background until we heed the call to listen, so we can upgrade the stories we have been told about ourselves. The skills to undertake this book were learnt along the way. And with each step I gained more insight into the reasons behind the legacy of literacy I am creating. I had to move beyond the fear of thinking I would be seen as stupid and trust that life had my back.

We are here to evolve and part of that is not to see ourselves as broken, but on a journey of developing and learning new skills and updating our abilities and integrating the soul and human essences. Your life is the teacher and mystery school and will call you to deepen into the human experience, to see beyond it being just mundane activity. I could so easily have stayed stuck in the limited stories of my life, what it means to be a traumatised woman lacking in mothering skills. But I chose to see that life was calling me into something deeper. Something that would later become my gift to so many.

BIBLIOGRAPHY/ FURTHER READING

I want to state that although I speak of many schools of learning that I ventured down in order to gain aspects of insight about myself, I have since let go of some of these teachings, however I feel it's important to highlight the lineages where some of my wisdom came from and was activated by.

BOOKS

Bethany Webster. *Discovering the Inner Mother: A Guide to Healing the Mother Wound and Claiming your Personal Power.* Harper Collins, 2021.

Black Girl Bliss. *Pussy Prayers: Sacred and Sensual Rituals for Wild Women of Color,* Eleven25 Media, 2018.

Elaine N. Aron. *The Highly Sensitive Person: How to Thrive When the World Overwhelms You.* Thorsons, 2017.

Emmi Mutale et al. *Return to The Mother World: Ancient Feminine Wisdom in Times of Transition.* Ama Publishing, 2023

Fleur Leussink. *Moving Beyond: Access your Intuition, Psychic Ability and Spirit Connection.* Yellow Kite Books, 2021.

Jane Astara Ashley (Edited and compiled by). *Sovereign unto Herself: Release Co-Dependencies and Claim your Authentic Power – essays from feminine thought leaders.* Flower of Life Press, 2020.

Jane Meredith. *Journey to the Dark Goddess: How to Return to your Soul.* Moon Books. 2017

Monica Sjöö & Barbara Mor. *The Great Cosmic Mother: Rediscovering the Religion of the Earth.* Harper One, 1991.

Neale Donald Walsch. *Conversations with God.* Hodder & Stoughton, 2009.

Penny Kellie. *Robes: A Book of Coming Changes*. Lily Hill Publishing, 2005.

Rebecca Campbell. *Rise Sister Rise: A Guide to Unleashing the Wise, Wild Woman Within*. Hay House, 2016.

Dr Shakti Mari Malan. *Sexual Awakening for Women: A Tantric Workbook*. Self published by Shakti, 2013.

Val Sampson. *Tantra: The Art of Mind-Blowing Sex*. Vermillion, 2004.

Valerie X Scott. *Surrogate Wife: The Story of a Masters and Johnson Sexual Therapist and the Nine Cases she Treated*. 1971

JOURNALS/PAPERS

David Hartman and Diane Zimberoff. "The Nourishment Barrier: The Shock Response to Toxic Intimacy". *Journal of Heart-Centered Therapies*, 2012, Vol. 15, No. 2, pp. 3-26.

James Gallagher. "Scientists grow whole model human embryo without sperm or egg," bbc.co.uk, September 6, 2023.

PODCASTS

Feminine Revered: Sacred Feminine Power Podcast – Emmi Mutale.

TRAININGS

Nectar Vulva and Vagina Mapping – created by Carly Rae Beaudry

Sacred Woman Awakening – Diana Beaulieu

The Authentic School of Tantra – founded by Devi Ward Erickson

Womb Sauna – founded by Thema Azize Serwa

ABOUT THE AUTHOR

Coco Oya Cienna-Rey is a UK-based mother, grandmother, creative, mystic, soul guide and writer. Her creativity is informed by her journey as a devotee of the Tantric path (an embodied path of self-liberation) and her personal journey with trauma. She has always felt a call to channel the Voice of the Divine Feminine and is published in several bestselling anthologies. Often thought provoking, yet always heartfelt her work speaks of the sacred wisdom stored in the body, the non-linear nature of trauma and the embodiment of soul. She believes that our innate connection to the natural world can heal humanity.

As a deeply sensitive, highly empathic gifted intuitive Coco can be found weaving her soul-coaching embodiment work at creativelycoco.com

ABOUT THE ARTIST

Dorrie Joy lives and works as a prolific multi-disciplinary artist. She teaches ancestral skills and traditional crafts and is also a herbalist, forager, poet, writer, international speaker and ceremonial leader.

As a painter, she is largely self taught. Her formal studies are in literature and ceramics.

For almost thirty years she has been initiated by and trained intimately with indigenous women and Elders in many areas of ancient craft and ceremony.

Her paintings are held in private collections and public displays and her ceremonial craft is carried and respected globally.

She has travelled widely and lives in the south west of the UK. A mother of three and a grandmother of two, her work is informed by her passion for sustainability, rooted in connection and reciprocity.

ABOUT WOMANCRAFT

Womancraft Publishing was founded on the revolutionary vision that women and words can change the world. We act as midwife to transformational women's words that have the power to challenge, inspire, heal and speak to the silenced aspects of ourselves.

We believe that:

- books are a fabulous way of transmitting powerful transformation,
- values should be juicy actions, lived out,
- ethical business is a key way to contribute to conscious change.

At the heart of our Womancraft philosophy is fairness and integrity. Creatives and women have always been underpaid. Not on our watch! We split royalties 50:50 with our authors. We work on a full circle model of giving and receiving: reaching backwards, supporting TreeSisters' reforestation projects, and forwards via Worldreader, providing books at no cost to education projects for girls and women.

We are proud that Womancraft is walking its talk and engaging so many women each year via our books and online. Join the revolution! Sign up to the mailing list at womancraftpublishing.com and find us on social media for exclusive offers:

- womancraftpublishing
- womancraft_publishing
- womancraftpublishing.com/books

USE OF WOMANCRAFT WORK

Often women contact us asking if and how they may use our work. We love seeing our work out in the world. We love you sharing our words further. And we ask that you respect our hard work by acknowledging the source of the words.

We are delighted for short quotes from our books – up to 200 words – to be shared as memes or in your own articles or books, provided they are clearly accompanied by the author's name and the book's title.

We are also very happy for the materials in our books to be shared amongst women's communities: to be studied by book groups, discussed in classes, read from in ceremony, quoted on social media…with the following provisos:

- If content from the book is shared in written or spoken form, the book's author and title must be referenced clearly.

- The only person fully qualified to teach the material from any of our titles is the author of the book itself. There are no accredited teachers of this work. Please do not make claims of this sort.

- If you are creating a course devoted to the content of one of our books, its title and author must be clearly acknowledged on all promotional material (posters, websites, social media posts).

- The book's cover may be used in promotional materials or social media posts. The cover art is copyright of the artist and has been licensed exclusively for this book. Any element of the book's cover or font may not be used in branding your own marketing materials when teaching the content of the book, or content very similar to the original book.

- No more than two double page spreads, or four single pages of any book may be photocopied as teaching materials.

We are delighted to offer a 20% discount of over five copies going to one address. You can order these on our webshop, or email us. If you require further clarification, email us at: info@womancraftpublishing.com

ALSO FROM WOMANCRAFT

Burning Woman

Lucy H. Pearce

Burning Woman is a breath-taking and controversial woman's journey through history – personal and cultural – on a quest to find and free her own power.

Uncompromising and all-encompassing, Lucy H. Pearce uncovers the archetype of the Burning Women of days gone by – Joan of Arc and the witch trials, through to the way women are burned today in cyber bullying, acid attacks, shaming and burnout, fearlessly examining the roots of Feminine power – what it is, how it has been controlled, and why it needs to be unleashed on the world during our modern Burning Times.

Burning Woman explores:

- Burning from within: a woman's power – how to build it, engage it and not be destroyed by it.
- Burning from without: the role of shame, and honour in the time-worn ways the dominant culture uses fire to control the Feminine.
- The darkness: overcoming our fear of the dark, and discovering its importance in cultivating power.

This incendiary text was written for women who burn with passion, have been burned with shame, and who at another time, in another place, would have been burned at the stake. With contributions from leading burning women of our era: Isabel Abbott, ALisa Starkweather, Shiloh Sophia McCloud, Molly Remer, Julie Daley, Bethany Webster…

Descent & Rising: Women's Stories & the Embodiment of the Inanna Myth

Carly Mountain

> *"The heroine is one who has remembered, reclaimed and reconnected with her unfettered red thread. She has been initiated into the spirit of the depths by her dark sister, and walks with newfound, embodied authority into the upperworld."*

What if, despite the uniqueness of your own life and experiences, each stage of the process of descent was universal? The journey of *Descent & Rising* is the core initiation of the feminine – the heroine's journey – one travelled by billions of women before you.

Descent & Rising explores real stories of women's descents into the underworld of the psyche – journeys of dissolution, grief and breakdown precipitated by trauma, fertility issues, loss of loved ones, mental health struggles, FGM, sexual abuse, birthing experiences, illness, war, burnout…

This is territory that Carly Mountain, psychotherapist and women's initiatory guide, knows intimately, and guides us through with exquisite care and insight, using the ancient Sumerian myth of the goddess Inanna as a blueprint. She maps not only the descent but the rising and familiarises us with a process of female psycho-spiritual growth overlooked in patriarchal culture.

> *"The heroine's journey is an erotic, mystical initiation that revivifies our place in the shape of things… The fodder of our descents provides the compost from which the richest fruits of our lives can grow. If only we can turn towards our pain and let it work in us."*

The Mistress of Longing

Wendy Havlir Cherry

The Mistress of Longing is…

An invitation to listen and trust the deep feminine that longs to be heard.
A love letter from, and for, devotion.
A prescription for a passionate and creative life.
A sacred reclamation.
A liberation of desire.
A hymn to kindness.
The voice of a modern mystic.

Mother in the Mother: looking back, looking forward – women's reflections on maternal lineage

Pippa Grace

Diverse, rich, celebratory, challenging, sometimes painful and ultimately uplifting together the stories in Mother in the Mother illuminate how the strength of maternal love can have the power to heal and overcome adversity.

Whilst much has been written about the complexity of the mother/daughter relationship, *Mother in the Mother* explores new territory by looking at the three-way relationship between grandmother, mother and child. Featuring the voices of over 50 mothers from a diverse range of ages, cultural backgrounds and experiences exploring themes of: love, stress, loss, healing, belonging, infertility, mental and physical health issues, twin pregnancy, adoption, pre-maturity, sexuality, single motherhood, young motherhood, abortion, maternal ambiguity and long-distance relationships with families of birth.